PRAISE WORKS!

Merlin R. Carothers

PRAISE WORKS!
Copyright 1973 by Merlin R. Carothers
Escondido, CA 92033-2518
www.foundationofpraise.org
All rights reserved
Printed in the United States of America
ISBN 10: 0-943026-06-7
ISBN 13: 978-0-943026-06-0

Other Best-Selling Books
By
MERLIN R. CAROTHERS

Prison to Praise
Power in Praise
Answers to Praise
Walking and Leaping
Bringing Heaven Into Hell
Victory on Praise Mountain
The Bible on Praise
More Power to You
What's on Your Mind?
Let Me Entertain You
From Fear to Faith
You Can Be Happy Now
Secret Sins
God's Secret Weapon
Amazing Power of Faith

Preface

Not every prisoner is a criminal sentenced for a violation of the law. Not every prison is made of stone and steel.

The hard, black, cold bars of mental facilities surround some of the blackest prisons in the world. They are like solid granite mountains, immovable and permanent. Millions of people are locked up, and many are tied down, in these monuments of man's failure to find the solution for mental agony.

Millions of others - you may be one of them - are not locked up in an actual physical building, but are imprisoned just as surely in prisons of their own making. They are so bound by their fears and frustrations, their problems and angers, their unforgivingness and unbelief, that they cannot enjoy the liberty Christ died to give them, nor the abundant life He promised to those who would take hold of it by faith.

But there is relief. There is a way out of even the darkest prisons of despair and self-pity. Miracles are happening today. I could tell you of thousands, but I must limit this book to only a few illustrations of what God is doing for people today.

Prisons of all kinds are being invaded with praise. Your prison, whatever its form, can be removed, and you can be transformed by a joy that is beyond your understanding. Learn the secret of freedom through praise and you may see your situation change. Better yet, you yourself will be changed, never to be a prisoner again. Freedom is real. Freedom is forever. Freedom comes through praise.

Stand fast therefore in the liberty wherewith Christ hath made us free, and be not entangled again with the yoke of bondage (Galations 5:1 KJV).

HEY, GOD!

Frank Foglio, author of *Hey, God!* and an International Director of the Full Gospel Business Men, told me one of the most remarkable accounts of deliverance through praise I have ever heard.

Frank's daughter was in a terrible automobile accident. Her head was severely injured, and although many thousands of prayers were made for her recovery, her mental condition grew steadily worse. Finally, she had to be placed in the "hopeless" ward at an institution. It was the very end of the line.

Patients in the ward were so far removed from reality that their families seldom came to visit them. One patient had been strapped down for twelve years! Others sat passively, staring at nothing, their vacant eyes reflecting minds emptied of all knowing. Still others lay rigid in beds, without sight or motion. Vegetables. Frank's daughter had clawed her way out of strait jackets and tried to hang herself with a bed sheet.

It had been seven years since the accident,

and the absolute hopelessness of his daughter's condition began to take its toll on a very tough Italian. Frank's faith in God started to waver.

On one very difficult trip to the institution, Frank was arguing with God.

"How could You be a God of love? I wouldn't let such a thing happen to my daughter if I had the power to prevent it. You could heal her. But You won't. Don't You love people as much as even I do? You must not." Frank felt his anger rising against God.

"Praise Me," a Voice said to him.

"What for?" Frank replied.

"Praise Me that your daughter is where she is."

"Never!" he spit out. "I would rather die than do that." God had no right to ask him to praise Him when God wasn't doing His own job of showing His love for people.

Frank remembered hearing a tape about giving thanks for all things. He had been deeply moved by the message, but at that moment he was in no mood to put it into practice.

"Thank Me that your daughter is exactly where she is," the Voice said again.

"God, I couldn't praise You if I tried. I'm not going to try, because I don't believe I should."

As Frank continued toward the facility, the Holy Spirit worked in his heart, and he felt his attitude begin to soften. He said, "Well, God, I would praise You if I could - but I just can't."

A little further along, he confessed, "I would praise You, but You would have to help me."

After arriving at the institution, Frank went through the necessary procedures to get clearance into the most restricted part of the building. It always took a long while to get into his daughter's ward. Sometimes, he wondered why he continued to come. His daughter didn't recognize him. She didn't know him from a stone on the ground.

Finally, Frank was in the last waiting room, the one that separated him from his daughter's ward. One steel door remained to be opened. Standing before it, Frank Foglio heard the calm, firm voice of God one more time:

"Thank Me that your daughter is exactly where she is."

The disobedience, the unwillingness, the hardness of heart had melted away. The stony heart of anger and bitterness and unbelief had somehow been replaced by a responsive heart of flesh. Frank, his throat choked with emotion, whispered his surrender:

"Okay, God. I thank You that my daughter is where she is. I know that You love her more than I do."

Then a vaguely familiar voice cried out; "I

want my daddy, I want my daddy."

The attendant opened the door, and Frank raced to his daughter's compartment. She threw out her arms and embraced her father.

"Daddy, where have you been?"

Nurses, attendants, and guards gathered around, weeping with joy.

Frank says, "Tell everyone our daughter is home now with us. We know that God always wants us to praise Him, no matter how things look."

My Comments

It took Frank only a few minutes to tell his story, and it took only a few minutes for you to read it. But try to picture the seven long years of anxiety, frustration, tears and fearful prayers. God saw their need from the very beginning, and longed to meet it, but He had to wait patiently - to let them learn what they needed to know.

One day Frank walked with his daughter to the platform of our church in Escondido, California. Her shining face and happy laughter were a testament of joy to the congregation. The Holy Spirit of God caused praise to rise within me.

"Oh, thank You, God, for teaching me the deliverance You have provided through praise.

Help me to share this glorious good news with the whole world."

You may be laboring over your own problem, nearly ready to give up. How long have you been struggling to find an answer? How great has your pain been? God has a perfect solution to your problem. He will move heaven and earth for you at the right time, and in the right way. Praise Him, trust Him, believe Him!

Happy is the man whom God correcteth: therefore despise not thou the chastening of the Almighty: For he maketh sore, and bindeth up: he woundeth, and his hands make whole. He shall deliver thee in six troubles; yea, in seven there shall no evil touch thee (Job 5:17-19 KJV).

FROM AN ATTORNEY

Fourteen years ago at age forty-two, I was the D.A. of our county and a practicing alcoholic. I still had my wife, although our marriage was shot. My wife says the only reason that we stayed together was because one or both of us were always too drunk to pack. In trying to find some answers for myself, I had purchased a Revised Standard Version of the Bible and a *Halley's Bible Handbook*. I used to sit with the Bible, the reference book, and a fifth of whiskey. When the whiskey was gone, I would curse because the Bible held no answers for me. About this time I was getting up to attend an early Bible study breakfast held at a restaurant. I usually showed up very belligerent, with a terrific hangover. Surprisingly enough, the men attending never threw me out, although they must have wanted to.

I started praying to whatever power caused the earth to turn, the tides to come and go, and the rain to fall, that He would help me stop drinking. I came to believe that He was helping me, and after a few months, I made a decision for Christ. I was so overjoyed with what the Lord was doing for me that I tried to share with everyone. Many of them thought I was ridiculous. I just couldn't keep quiet so I started sharing with prisoners in the jail. The Holy Spirit converted many of these prisoners.

Because I was so nervous during my first year of sobriety, I used to ask God every day to make me less nervous. After a year of sobriety, I was in Portland at an AA meeting. I mentioned that despite my prayers, I was more nervous after a year's sobriety than I had been before. One lady said, "Don't worry about it. Many members in Portland had the same experience. They called it *Frantic serenity.*"

The thought came to me that maybe I'd

been going about this thing the wrong way. I remembered that during the war I had used nervous energy to keep going when the other men could not. I decided that being nervous was a gift from God, and I should be thanking Him instead of demanding that He change me.

So I started thanking God every day for being so nervous - and that is when a miracle took place. I became calm with my nervousness. This summer I read *Prison to Praise* and *Power in Praise*, and understood what the Holy Spirit had taught me.

About a month ago, I had an absolutely disastrous week in court, losing three cases in a row. I said, "Lord, I don't see how this can possibly work out for the good of my clients, but thank You anyway." And since then I have seen clear evidence in each case, that it is working for my clients' good!

My Comments

Lawyers, doctors, and specialists in many fields are stepping forward to say, "Praise works." Unbelievers are forced to take another look at God's promises. The reactions vary, but in some way they are all saying, "It sounds absolutely crazy, but praising God for everything turned my disastrous life into an incredible new experience."

Peace I leave with you; My own peace I give and bequeath to you (John 14:27 AMP).

I WOULDN'T BELIEVE IT

A friend of mine sent me a copy of *Prison to Praise*. I read and enjoyed it, but I warned other readers to be careful, as it could be taken wrong. I could not bring myself to thank God for something He did not cause. I know sickness, sorrow, and pain are from the enemy.

Then I became ill. I went to a physician and learned I had gall bladder trouble.

This was Monday. The next day, your book *Power in Praise* was given to me. I could hardly put it down, but I kept saying to myself, "I will not say it, I will not say it."

I cried at some incident in each chapter. I could tell the Holy Spirit was speaking to me.

Finally I said, "Thank You, Lord, for my gall bladder," and He said, "What gall bladder?" I began to cry all the more, and had to quit reading as I could not see.

Later I returned to the book and read where a couple had thanked God for their totally psychotic daughter. I thought, "If they can thank God for her being completely insane, I can surely muster up enough courage to thank

Him for my bad gall bladder." Still weeping, I managed to cry out, "Thank You, Lord, for my bad gall bladder."

Instantly, the pain began to leave! I had been rebelling against God! I was rebelling against the Truth of His Word. I thank the Lord for this "new" idea that is 2,000 years old. In my rebellion, I had refused to see it.

My Comments

There are many things that we can refuse to see in God's Word. We often decide what we want to believe and cling to - no matter what His Word says. God has promised to bless anyone who will trust Him. Are you willing to believe that He can bless even you?

Is there anything of which it may be said, "See, this is new"? It has already been (Ecclesiastes 1:10 AMP).

WORD OF MOUTH

I shall never be able to thank God enough for allowing me to attend three of your services. Your message on praising God has changed my whole life. Although I had been a Spirit-filled Christian for many years, since hearing you,

I've been able to have victory over problems that had gone on for thirty years!

My Comments

Reading about praising God does help us, but hearing about it from others can have an even greater effect. You can let the praise of your lips influence the lives of those around you. You may be amazed at the hundreds of opportunities you can find every day to say, "Thank You, Lord," for all the little things that happen. Your praise will be contagious to those around you, and they will pass it on to others. Your casual, yet intentional praise, can spread around the world.

Faith comes from hearing the message... (Romans 10:17 NIV).

I WAS A WRECK

It is 2:30 am, and I have just finished reading *Power in Praise*.

My parents divorced in 1951 when I was three years old. I grew up an emotional cripple, with a lovely facade to hide it all. In desperation and loneliness, I married a boy I did not love, could not love, because I was a lesbian.

The marriage ended in divorce, but only after I had borne a child. I received custody of our son.

I was content, financially secure, and had no need, or desire for God. I blew pot and took LSD. As a result, I lost my job and spent a month in an institution. Since that day, almost a year ago, my "bad luck" increased.

Last January I was baptized in the Holy Spirit and delivered from homosexuality! I was happy and thankful - temporarily. Then I turned away from God, and my worldly problems overwhelmed me again. Bills and trouble have piled up in irritating stacks. I have no job, no prospects, and no money.

A few hours ago, I was in a charismatic prayer meeting and was given your book. I didn't feel any better for having gone to the meeting, but when I started reading your book, my heart began to change. I read a few pages and cried and read some more and cried some more. Now I know why I'm in such a mess. Rebellious as I have been, God had to break me to draw me back to Himself. I tearfully begged His forgiveness and thanked Him for the circumstances that have brought me back. There aren't words to describe my joy.

My Comments

What a beautiful testimony of the love of God reaching down to redeem the lost. Frequently we cannot understand what God is doing, or permitting to happen. Please learn wisdom from this letter and apply it in your own life. Instead of fear and impatience, believe that God is working for your good. He will take whatever Satan is doing to you, or to your loved ones, and use it to bless and help you. God will not force our obedience, but He will use circumstances to help us make a right choice.

PS: It has been several months since this woman entered a life of praise. She says her joy and strength are increasing.

These (trials) have come so that your faith... may be proved genuine and may result in praise, glory and honor when Jesus Christ is revealed (I Peter 1:7 NIV).

HE NEEDED HELP

A man in our office was in trouble, but he didn't know it. He was very well educated, thought he knew more than the boss did, and frequently made his attitude known to the boss himself. It was evident to me that the boss was disgusted with this man.

If he were to be fired, I knew the man would

fall apart. He had more problems than anyone I've ever known. His wife had divorced him and taken nearly everything he had. He was a sexual deviate; his nerves were so bad his hands would shake when he was perturbed about anything; his stomach was upset all the time; he was an alcoholic; and - I could go on and on.

I felt very sorry for this man, and I prayed for him daily, but he continued to get worse. He was demoted to a very inferior position, but had no understanding that it was his own fault.

Your book, *Prison to Praise*, was given to me, and I decided to try praising God for this man. I thanked God for the man as he was, and I believed God would use his problems to help him. I heard the Lord speak to me as I had never heard Him before! He said, "Go to his church, and pray for him."

"But Lord," I protested, "he is Catholic, and I am Protestant. "

"Go to his church and pray."

So, to his church I went. It was the United Nations Catholic Chapel in New York. Everything was very strange to me, but while praying, I experienced a wonderful joy and peace that God was going to help that man. God must have really lit my face up, for the priest sent someone to ask who I was.

When I returned to the office the next day,

to my amazement I heard the man saying to the boss, "I'm sorry, sir. I made a mistake." He had never before shown any humility. From that day on, his attitude and conduct continued to change for the better. I'm excited about the idea of praising the Lord for people as they are.

My Comments

People with every problem we can think of, surround us. Our natural reaction is to avoid those who have the greatest needs. They are obnoxious, arrogant, weak, or act as if they do not want our help. But if they come to our attention, God has a specific reason for bringing them into our lives. Seeing that they need help takes no love on our part. However, if we learn to thank the Lord for them, as they are, He will release His love in us to help them. Please do not turn away from those you dislike. They are God's gift to you. They will help you learn about Christ's love. When you feel irritation rising within you, let the power of praise counteract it. Jesus will use your praise to meet their needs. And your own distress will be turned to joy, as you see God working.

Whenever anyone gives himself over to rejoicing and thanking God for all things, miracles happen. Gifts of the Spirit begin to be manifested in that person. Praise for and to God literally opens the way for the Holy Spirit to bring new insight and understanding to us.

In the above case, the writer was given a spiritual insight that enabled her to help another person.

Every good and perfect gift is from above, coming down from the Father (James 1:17 NIV).

DELIBERATE SIN

This is the first time that I have ever really thought about praising God for all things. I am still puzzled by one thing: Should we praise Him for sin in our lives? If I, through a rebellious or negligent heart, sin, I have gone against God's plan for my life, haven't I? He didn't want me to sin, did He?

For example, I know I should be meeting with the Lord every day in His Book and in prayer. That requires discipline on my part. But if I, because I don't feel like it, decide not to have my quiet time that day, I am sinning. So, how can I praise God for not having my devotions? If I deliberately neglect to do what He has commanded, shouldn't I be asking God for forgiveness?

Maybe what I'm saying is that praising God

implies that it wasn't my fault, that He wanted it to happen to me. But does God want sin in our lives?

Another example, an extreme one. If I deliberately plotted to kill someone, went out and did it, how could I praise God for that?

I can see praising God for the fact that my car conks out. But can I really praise Him if it conked out because I deliberately refused to put gas in it?

Really, I am confused. Is there anything you can say that would answer some of these questions?

There is one area in my life where Satan continually bugs me and that's my immoral past. I'm now twenty-one, and am attending a university. God moved in my life in a great way about two years ago and I committed my life to Him as best as I knew how. Until that time, I had not been the purest of women. I want to forget that. God has forgiven me for those things, but Satan keeps bringing these experiences into my mind. It says in Colossians three and Philippians four (and many other places) that we should set our mind on godly things. I try to do this. But I must admit that Satan sometimes wins.

I would appreciate it, and thank the Lord, if you would pray that Christ will have victory in these areas of my life. I don't want to sin.

My Comments

I know that it sounds really strange to praise God for sin in our lives. But if we fail to praise God for one thing, we open wide the door to fail to praise Him for many things. Once we determine that we will praise Him for all things, a major victory has been won.

It is true that we may have to suffer in this life for the sins that we commit. But there is another glorious reality about sin. It points to our urgent need of Christ's forgiveness. The less we understand that He forgives us, the more inclined we are to proceed in our old sinful way of life. However, the more we believe He forgives us, the more we want to flee from sin.

Ideally, devotions should not be an act of obedience to God. Devotions are an opportunity to hear from our Lord who loves us, and to talk with Him. Until we understand this, devotions will never be an enjoyable part of our lives. Can you imagine how strained a love relationship would be if they felt as though they were *obligated* to read the letters written to one another? God does not want our obligation; He wants our love.

If a person were deliberately plotting to murder someone, they could not honestly praise God. If following the act they realized their sin, and asked for God's forgiveness, He could use that terrible sin to work out something good. He used the murder of His own Son to bring salvation to mankind.

She is afraid that she is breaking God's laws, is unworthy of His love, and does not have the right to praise Him for everything. But the more we praise God for our weaknesses or failures, the less we will want to do these things. It is clear that feeling guilty has not helped her. Physical acts, whatever they may be, are never as likely to separate us from God as our lack of love for Him.

Satan cannot stand an atmosphere of worship and praise to God. Anytime we thank God for our weaknesses, a marvelous power is released to help us receive Christ's strength in their place. Never use praise as an excuse for sin. Use sin as a reason for praise.

This is a faithful saying and worthy of all acceptance, that Christ Jesus came into the world to save sinners of whom I am chief (I Timothy 1:15 NKJV).

SICK, SICK, SICK

A remark you made in *Answers to Praise* prompts me to write. You said, "If praying has left you with nothing but discouragement, try the prayer of praise and thanksgiving."

I don't want this to be a completely negative letter, but I have to tell it like it is. I am going through a terrible time. I see my personality and character disintegrating. Despair and worry are killing me.

My daughter has an affliction that does not allow her to grow or develop as a young girl should. She is only four feet seven and is almost seventeen years old. She is lonely, feels rejected, and is emotionally disturbed. She doesn't have a single friend. She is home alone, seven nights and days a week. Surely this is not a loving God's plan for her. She has to take hormones for the rest of her life, and we know hormones are dangerous.

Now, how do I pray? Do I thank God for her affliction, for her loneliness, for her unhappiness? Do I thank God for her misery and complete lack of the normal fun and companionship she so longs for? Please, please, how do I pray, what do I say? Our Lord Jesus did not like to see illness and unhappiness, and He healed.

Please help me out of this web of confusion and hopelessness. There is so much in the way. My relationship with my husband is empty, and I'm always dogged by feelings of guilt. That's fine if the Holy Spirit is convicting me, but along with conviction I need help.

I really don't know how to pray anymore. I love Jesus, but I am far from Him. Only God can help my family and me. Can you tell me what is wrong? Something is holding me back, but what? Please, if you can, tell me what I need to do and how to pray and I'll do it.

My Comments

Jesus hung on the cross alone, betrayed, rejected and hated. He suffered an agony of body and soul that few humans could understand. But what does that do for us? His suffering was to provide each one of us with health, as well as the joy and peace that are unmoved by circumstances. He wants us to receive them. But we must believe that He is using our problems to help us, so that our faith in Jesus can begin to grow.

Up to this point, this woman has chosen to think about everything bad. She must chose now to praise God for His love and for the gift of His Son seventy times-seven times every day. When a fearful or unhappy thought comes, we can reject it, replacing it with thanksgiving for sight, hearing, limbs, lungs - everything we can think of. What had been a sad, unlovely disposition, will begin to shine.

Our friends and family will notice. Nothing is so beautiful as a woman filled with praise to God. Our praise can open the door to healing for our entire family!

Remember this, God feels our pain. He understands and wants to help us. He is limited only by our faith to believe Him! As we praise Him, our faith and joy will grow. Our testimony will then reach many others.

He (Jesus) is able for all time to save those who draw near to God through Him, since He always lives to make intercession for them (Hebrews 7:25 RSV).

CANCER AND LEUKEMIA

I have read your book, *Prison to Praise*, and I can't resist writing to let you know how much it has helped me.

When I was ten years old, my father killed my mother. He was sent to prison, and I to live with an aunt and uncle. I married when I was twenty. At twenty-two I lost my husband to cancer, but I was blessed with his child. Now, six years later, my present husband and I have been told that our daughter has leukemia. The news shattered me. I didn't see how I could face two bouts with that dreaded disease.

My first urge was to race home and kill myself, but before I got home, my plan left my mind. I returned to the hospital with an overpowering urge to talk to our preacher. He came at once and offered us his help. That night at church I went down front asking for special prayer. During the prayer session, I forgave my father for killing my mother and prayed that he would receive peace of mind.

I have been praying for our daughter's total recovery, but until I read your book, I was not praising God for these trials. I've now got a new understanding of God and His will. Thank you for sharing your experiences.

My Comments

When we try to carry the burdens of tragedies in our lives, Satan will often suggest, "Go ahead and kill yourself." However, if we turn these problems over to God, His Spirit will suggest, "Be at peace. I will abundantly supply everything that you need." The sick often say, "But where is God when I need Him most?" He is there urging us to give our problem to Him. When we praise Him, our faith releases His power to supply the grace and peace we need. This letter illustrates the deliverance from fear and anger that God wants to give each of His children. The problem itself may remain, but the result is that we are victorious through Jesus, who strengthens us.

And my God will meet all your needs according to His glorious riches in Christ Jesus (Philippians 4:19 NIV).

GRIN AND BEAR IT

I heard you speak in St. Louis in August of 1970 at a Full Gospel Businessmen's convention. When you began speaking, I gritted my teeth. I had a preconceived idea of what a message by an Army Colonel would be like. I settled back in my seat, prepared to grin and bear it, not too happy about the whole matter. Then, much to my surprise, you really caught my interest. Your message was quite long, but not nearly long enough to suit me. I wanted you to go on for hours. My preconceived ideas went out the window. Your message left a greater impression on me than any I had ever heard.

I bought your book, *Prison to Praise*, and it changed my life. I began praising God for everything, both good and bad, and as I did my joy and peace increased. It's so much better to be happy and thankful than unhappy and complaining.

My Comments

Yes,being thankful for everything is very difficult to grasp - and so is atomic energy. Yet most people believe in atomic power, because they have heard about it from sources they consider reliable. At least a million people in our own country, and thousands around the world, are declaring that praising God is setting them free from pain they had struggled with for many years. If it works, why not use it?

A happy heart is a good medicine and a cheerful mind works healing (Proverbs 17:22 AMP).

ELECTRIC POLISHER

I have postponed writing this letter for over a month for two reasons: (1) I wanted to make sure that the spectacular change that has taken place in my life, because of following your advice to praise God in everything, was not just a fluke or one of those "highs" that happen in the Christian life; (2) Once thoroughly convinced that this was not a passing thing, I haven't been able to think of words in which I could adequately express my appreciation to you for yielding yourself to God so that He could use you to tell us these truths.

I could go on for pages, but I'll spare you that. I would like, however, to tell you of one incident that happened. About four or five days after I began to take seriously this business of praising God in everything, I was working at my business polishing and waxing cars for dealers, and getting them ready for sale. The electric buffer I was using snatched the heavy chrome strip off the side of a car and wound it up around the "wheel" of the buffer like a clock spring. The end of the strip slapped my right wrist at 2800 RPM. I couldn't shut the buffer off because the switch was defective, and I couldn't drop it. I had to go and pull the plug.

I suppose the end of the strip struck my wrist 400 or 500 times. It was *very* painful! Do you know what I found myself saying while this was going on? "Praise the Lord, Thank You, Jesus." I would no more have expected to praise God under those circumstances than to be dancing a jig on top of a new car.

I was sure my wrist was ruined. I was particularly concerned because my left wrist has been "frozen," made entirely immobile by osteomyelitis, ever since I was thirteen. While one stiff wrist has never been any great handicap to me, the possibility of having two of them was not attractive.

Later, my right wrist had the worst pain I've

ever experienced. It lasted about two minutes, although it seemed like half an hour, and again I found myself saying, "Thank You, Jesus." My speaking could not have been more involuntary. It just came out of me. I believe in that moment God set and healed the broken bones in my wrist.

When the doctor x-rayed my wrist, she asked me if I had ever injured that wrist before. I told her that I hadn't, and she said, "That's very strange." There was evidence in the x-rays that some of the bones had been broken and healed. I have other problems in my life, but there is evidence that God is working in them, and I know that they are as good as done. I am thanking God for the solutions and enjoying being relieved of the burden of the problems. I don't know how He's going to work them out, but I know He will. Isn't He a wonder!

If I don't see you while I am in this dilapidated house in which I currently reside, I shall search for you near the Throne, so that I may express my love and gratitude.

My Comments

There is nothing complicated about simple faith in God. It only seems complicated because we, in our frustrations, make it so. Childlike faith is nothing more than believing that God has supplied our need before we see any evidence that He has done so.

Let all those rejoice who put their trust in You; let them ever shout for joy (Psalm 5:11 NKJV).

I DON'T UNDERSTAND

A friend gave me *Power in Praise* and *Prison to Praise*. I read every word, and have been expecting something to happen to me, too. I ask God to stop me from crying every day, and feeling sorry for myself, but nothing happens.

My husband divorced me after nineteen years of marriage. He was not much fun, but he was very good to me. We were together all the time. Now I am alone, sixty-one years old, and so lonely and miserable. I cry every day, and it does not help one bit.

I don't understand why so many good things happen to those people in your book and nothing good happens to me. What can I do? I still love my husband and can't get him out of my mind. The few friends I have left are tired of my crying. So am I. Could you please tell me what I can do? I have faith in the Lord, read the Bible every day, and go to church regularly.

My Comments

What can this dear lady do? My answer is, start believing that He is using every experience in her life to bring something good to her. Her faith will release all of God's power to do for her what He already wants to do! Our fears and anxieties are the very things that hold back His power.

She says, "I have faith in the Lord." This is exactly what God wants us to have, but what she does not have. As we praise Him-constantly-with every ounce of determination that we have, our confidence that God is going to use all of our experiences for our good will bring us into His joy.

We rejoice in our sufferings, knowing that suffering produces endurance, and endurance produces character, and character produces hope, and hope does not disappoint us, because God's love has been poured into our hearts through the Holy Spirit which has been given to us (Romans 5:3-5 RSV).

DISCOURAGED NUN

Praise be to God for your book, *Prison to Praise*. Until I read it, I was a discouraged

Catholic nun. I was seriously thinking of giving up this life, and God. But now, praising God for everything, I am happy and content in doing the work of the Lord. This joy and peace I feel is something I have never felt before. I am getting my pupils to praise God for everything, also. Thanks again for making my life beautiful. God bless you always.

My Comments

There are discouraged people in every occupation. But God is using praise to bring deliverance. He is enthroned with our praises, and delights to give us His joy and peace .

...Those who hope in Me will not be disappointed (Isaiah 49:23 NIV).

FROM PRISON

Praising the Lord for difficult circumstances revolutionized my life. I am in the county jail on a ten year probation violation and on a burglary charge. I also have a narcotics charge pending, but my worries, grudges, strains, and fears have disappeared through God's gift of praise.

When I first came to the county jail I was sick of life. I was here two weeks when I read

Prison to Praise. That same day I accepted Jesus Christ as my Savior and Lord, and received the wonderful Baptism in the Holy Spirit. A month later, I read *Power in Praise*, and that did it. Now my cell is filled with praise.

After reading *Prison to Praise* I was still a little confused about the power in praise, but when I read *Power in Praise*, my confusion disappeared. Life is so much more beautiful in this world, now that I have the Heavenly Father with me. The Lord has shown me that being confined in a reformatory twice before was also part of His plan. Please pray with us for the Lord's lost sheep who are in our tank here at the jail. Pray that they will have the courage to lay down their lives for Jesus Christ.

My Comments

If God can turn a jail cell into a place of praise and joy, how about the place where you live? Would you like to do something for the inmates of the more than two million jail cells in the United States? By providing copies of *Prison to Praise* the Foundation of Praise will help you do that. During 1972, thirty-five men were murdered inside the prisons of just one state. The power of God's Holy Spirit is needed to change lives in those places!

...I came that they may have life, and have it abundantly. I am the good Shepherd (John 10:10-11 RSV).

SON ON FIRE

I read your book and thought, "I could never praise God for my son being like he is. His dirty long hair, dirty clothes, won't get a job, and the drunkenness and drugs are too much for any mother to stand - let alone be thankful for." But a nagging thought kept churning in my mind: "Nothing else has worked; maybe God is trying to tell me something."

One night, some of my son's friends brought him home and carried him into our living room. They laid his unconscious, drunken body on the hearth in front of the fireplace. When they left, I sat in a chair and looked at him.

"God, how could I thank You for that?"

I heard, "I want you to thank Me."

"But I can't," was all I could say.

As I sat there looking at him, and shaking my head in despair, I saw smoke rising from my son! The flames in the fireplace had caught his clothes on fire! I ran over and smothered the blaze with my hands. While my hands were still on him, I had an overpowering urge to pray.

Okay, God. I thank You for my son exactly as he is." I wept as I prayed. To my surprise, my son sat straight up and said, "Mother, did you mean that?"

"Yes, I did son."

He went off to bed. The next morning I saw him in the bathroom with a big pair of scissors, cutting off his dirty hair. Why are you doing that?" I asked him. "I'm going to try to get a job, and I know I can't get one unless I cut some of this off." What a surprise that was! In the afternoon, he came back and said, "I haven't found a job yet, but I remembered something I want to do." He went into his bedroom and brought out two handfuls of materials he said were for taking drugs. I don't know if I can change, mother, but I have a strong urge to try to be what you want me to be."

My Comments

God can do in a moment of time what parents could not accomplish in years of criticism, complaining, or urging. Parents may want many things from their children, but only God can change a human being. He can take everything - even the bad - and use it to help those we love. He may not always do it in the twinkling of an eye, but He has His own perfect time schedule.

With men this is impossible, but with God all things are possible (Matthew 19:26 RSV).

THE WRATH OF GOD

I need your help. The church I attend has taught me nothing but the wrath and judgment of God. This has put me in great bondage and fear. I have no confidence in myself and no love for God. When I was younger, I loved God, but hearing about His wrath for so long has caused all love to leave me. It is difficult for me to explain how I can believe in God and yet not love Him. I know, from what Jesus said, that the most important thing is for me to love Him. What can I do if I don't love Him? Should I praise God that I don't love Him? I think of God as standing ready to punish me if I make a mistake. Please pray for me and give me any help that you can.

My Comments

The Bible tells us, in many places, that we are to fear God, for He is A Holy and Awesome God. In Proverbs, the fear of the Lord is described as the beginning of wisdom, as reverent awe, as hating evil and providing a long life. The only people who need to be in fear and terror of God, are those who reject Jesus.

Many people also have difficulty relating to God as a loving Heavenly Father, because their earthly father is so unloving. Whether our difficulty in loving God stems from personal experience or unbalanced teaching, the fact remains that God loved us enough to sacrifice His only Son to take away our sins. Why? So that He could bring many children - those of us who believe and trust His plan of salvation - to Himself. He did this because He loves us unconditionally.

If we have difficulty receiving God's love, we need to cry out to the Lord and ask Him to help us. The desire of God's heart is that we return His love, for He loves us infinitely beyond our ability to comprehend. God is faithful. He will help us as we cast ourselves upon His mercy.

Then those who feared the Lord talked often one to another, and the Lord listened and heard it, and a book of remembrance was written before Him of those who reverenced and worshipfully feared the Lord, and who thought on His Name. And they shall be Mine, says the Lord of Hosts, in that day when I publicly recognize and openly declare them to be My jewels (Malachi 3:16-17 AMP).

TRANSFORMED

The following letter is so unusual that you may find it difficult to believe. You may be offended by the writer's frankness, but her life-style is typical of a large segment of our American society.

I knew I needed God when I woke up in a mental ward with restraints on my arms and legs. I had tried to commit suicide.

I've never had any love except God's. I was adopted when I was three days old.

I am nineteen now. When I was thirteen, I had sex with my brother. I thank God I had a miscarriage, but the whole story came out, and everyone in our town knew about me. I've never been able to talk or write to anyone about this until now.

I got married when I was fifteen. I had open-heart surgery the same year. I had a baby at sixteen, and another at seventeen. My husband left after our second baby was born, and we've been separated since then.

I began hanging around with hippies, and I started taking downers. I had an operation to keep me from getting pregnant again, and sex became a part of every day of the week - usually with someone different each time.

I felt no one loved me, so I took a whole bottle

of sleeping pills, and ended up in the mental ward. In the hospital, I began to feel that there were people who cared about me. A nurse gave me your book, *Prison to Praise*. While reading it, I cried so much that my pillow was soaking wet. It became real to me that God loved me. It was tough to thank Him for my past life, but I did, and then He made me into a new person. What I used to be is not what I am now! I am thankful that regardless of what I was, God used your book to show me that He loves me.

My Comments

The agony of guilt and shame is usually more damaging to us than the act of sin itself. Self-torture drives many people to self-destruction. No matter how far from God any person is, he is transformed when he understands that God loves him.

Most people realize they are sinners. Nearly every down and out person I have ever known, knows he is bad. What he doesn't know is that God loves him enough to give him a new life, a brand new life that is free from all guilt. How can we feel guilt over something another person did? He took "upon Himself" our sin!

Therefore, if anyone is in Christ, he is a new creation; the old has passed away, behold, the new has come (II Corinthians 5:17 RSV).

I DISAGREE

I recently read two of your books. They are helpful and inspiring. However, I would take issue with a statement you made on page two of *Power in Praise* - "To praise God for a difficult situation (in this case a father's alcoholism) means we accept that it is part of God's plan to reveal His love to us." I don't believe God wants us to live a life of degradation. He gives us a free choice to seek His will, or to live in our own selfish fashion. How can God be blamed if we choose our own way? If we allow Him, He can and will direct us, and bring something wonderful out of any situation.

After finishing the book, I'm convinced this is your thinking, too, and that the wording is misleading. My brother-in-law, at sixty years of age, is a broken, unfulfilled, selfish man due to his choosing to drink alcoholic beverages. His health is poor after years of punishment to his body. He never sought God's guidance, and yet when his habit finally caught up with him, he blamed God. I believe it was a natural result of his disobedience, and that he is still buck-passing as he has done all these years. To say that this was God's will for his life is unthinkable. He had so many talents, so much to give others.

I am searching for a clear-cut understanding and would appreciate your comments.

We know that things work for good as long as God is directing our lives. So you see, I am not taking issue with all that you say, for it has opened up a new way of thinking, and I'm grateful beyond words. Life is sweeter, more relaxed, more meaningful with Him as the center of all things. Thank you so very much.

My Comments

I agree that people often disregard God's plan. This is the reason that I emphasize that all things work together for good to them that love God. If we do not love God and are not seeking His will, most of the things in our lives work against us and go against God's plan. However, I do know that God loves all men. Though they fight against Him and ruin their health, God is still trying to help them. Even acute alcoholism can be used by God to bring a person to accept Christ.

As we release our faith to believe God is working - even in the sad condition of alcoholism- His power is released to use the problem to draw a person to Christ. God will honor our faith. This does not mean that He approves, nor that we approve of sin; it simply means we are trusting Him to use everything to accomplish His purpose. We must not be discouraged that many do not immediately respond to His love. We may not understand, but we must trust that God knows every detail of our problems and desires to bring good out of Satan's evil schemes.

We believe that God can use even a wasted life to draw one more person to Christ. Jesus came into the world to find that one lost sheep. He is concerned over the ninety-nine, but gave His life for the one who wasted his own life in riotous living. As God used the sins of the prodigal son to bring him to his senses, He wants to use the experiences of all men to help them. Those who do not respond must fight against the love of God, and do so to their own destruction.

Rejoice with Me; for I have found My sheep which was lost (Luke 15:6 KJV).

A NURSE PRAYS

Due to strife in my marriage, I began to pray and read my Bible. I still didn't feel any great release, even after the problems began to straighten out, but I continued to read and pray.

I am a nurse, and I do private duty. One day I was taken from one case and placed with a Christian with terminal cancer. This wonderful Christian asked me if I had read *Prison to Praise*. I told her no, so she asked her family to bring it for me to read.

As the days and weeks passed, my patient grew weaker. Often she would lapse into a coma. Most of the time she didn't know I was there. Your book was in the room so I started reading it.

Due to the severity of my patient's illness, the room was kept in darkness. The window shades were taped down and the door was kept closed. No one entered the room except her doctor and the private duty nurses. I had opened a crack between the shade and window about one inch for enough light to read. The more I read, the more God dealt with my heart. Finally, I was led to get my Bible out of my pocketbook and fall on my knees to pray.

The Bible was a Testament my only son handed me the day he left home to attend college. He had been a Christian since he was twelve years old. With no help from me, he used to get up and go to Sunday school, leaving me asleep in bed. Other boys called him a square and a sissy because he carried his Bible in his car and tried to witness for Christ.

As I knelt with my Bible in my hands, suddenly the darkened room became as bright as if a powerful floodlight had been turned on. I turned around to see who had come into the room. No one was there, and the door was closed.

I started reading your book again, and this is what I read: "My son, what I want you to know is that you never again have to worry whether anyone will overcharge you, hurt you, or mistreat you, unless it is My will. Your life is in the palm of My hand. You can trust Me for all things. As you continue to thank Me in all circumstances, you will see how perfectly I work out every detail of your life." As I read those words I knew that Christ was my Savior.

All this happened about 1 p.m. The patient had not moved, or spoken on my shift, but the moment I accepted Christ she stirred and said, "Joyce, come hold my hand, and let's pray."

My son almost shouted when I telephoned and told him I had accepted Christ as my Savior. In his rejoicing, he said, "Mother, God has answered my prayers. I have been praying for you to become a Christian for many years."

Since then I have bought many copies of *Prison to Praise, Power in Praise* and *Answers to Praise.* I am praying that God will lead you to write more books. You have solved my Christmas shopping problem as I plan to give each one on my list your three books and a copy of the Living Bible. I only wish I had enough money to place a copy of *Prison to Praise* in every hospital room and jail cell in this town.

People who have known me for many years tell me that I even have a different facial expression from the one I used to have. I tell them I am so happy to have Jesus for my friend that I want to shout it to the world!

My Comments

Many are becoming known as "one of those people with a silly grin." A life of continual peace in Christ is intended for every child of God. He designs His promises for those who have problems! If you have felt "left out," start saying, "Praise You Lord." Thank and praise Him continually, and His Spirit will begin a new work in you.

Let the people praise thee, O God; let all the people praise thee (Psalm 67:5 KJV).

A CHAPLAIN RECEIVES

While I was in Vietnam, I was struck by the singular lack of power in my life. I believed in miracles, because if it hadn't been for the healing power of God, I would have died as a child. I preached on miracles and encouraged people to believe God for them, and God did answer some of our prayers in Vietnam, in a miraculous way. But somehow, I couldn't reach the drug addicts who were sincere in wanting and needing help. I would hear them ask Jesus to come into their hearts, but no changes were evident.

I prayed and read the Word faithfully. Then I read your book. It started me to praising God for some things, but questions of war and horrendous accidents among the men acted as a block. I didn't see how I could praise God for such things as that.

Then came the clincher. I got my orders assigning me to Fort Belvoir. I didn't want Fort Belvoir, Washington, D.C., or anywhere on the East Coast. I wanted Fort Lewis or Fort Ord on the West Coast. When I called my wife via overseas phone, she wept about the assignment.

Always before, I had believed that God led me in each assignment. Therefore, I never bothered anyone when my orders came through. This time I thought I would make an exception and go to the chief's office with some excuse and ask for re-assignment. But on the way to Fort Belvoir and the Washington area from San Francisco, I said, "No. I will leave this in the hands of God and thank Him." The post chaplain assigned me to the Religious Education/Hospital slot. I didn't like that. Religious Education was no favorite of mine, and I related poorly to medical personnel. But I was stuck with it.

One Monday, a Spirit-baptized Episcopalian woman came into my office to talk. She telephoned me later that day to say that I was going to be baptized in the Spirit within seven days.

"Great," I thought, "I'm a candidate for anything God has for me. He can whip it on me anytime." The next Sunday night, a Spirit-baptized couple came to our youth meeting and many young people were filled with the Holy Spirit. I thought that was fine.

"Let's just go up to the altar and praise God for what He has already done," I suggested.

We all went forward. I knelt, held my arms upward and said, "God, here I am at Your disposal. Use me any way You can." With that, two young people came up and said, "God has just showed us you are going to be baptized in the Holy Spirit. Do you mind if we lay hands on you and pray?"

"No. Go right ahead." They prayed, and I felt nothing. I thought, *Well, that's par for the course.* Then one of them said, "Let it out, let it out." I thought, *Let what out?*

"Let it go," they said.

Then I thought, *Well, if they want me to make funny sounds, I can do that for them.* I did, and still felt nothing.

They all said, "Praise God. He's received."

I wasn't sure what I had received. When they wanted to sing in tongues, I said to myself, *No way. This isn't of God.*

I doubted my experience for a week, but then decided that perhaps I should take what happened on faith.

In the middle of the week following the experience, the senior chaplain called me into his office and said, "You are relieved of your job. I do not want any Pentecostal influence around our young people."

Since then, the things I see God doing through me simply amaze me. I marvel at His love and mercy.

My mother and father now speak in tongues. A neighbor lady was healed of epilepsy and baptized in the Spirit. Fifteen young men gave their lives to Christ in a jail service. I don't know what effect this will have on my career as a chaplain, but then, that's not my business. I praise God I have learned that it's all His business.

My Comments

Learning and growing in praise leads to all kinds of fascinating experiences. We can never guess what God is going to do, or how He is going to do it. Many people step into the Baptism in the Holy Spirit when they start praising God for what is happening in their lives. Military chaplains are now receiving the Baptism in the Holy Spirit. A four-star Army general is traveling around the country telling chaplains they need to be baptized in the Holy Spirit. Unbelieving senior chaplains are forced to stand back and let God do "His thing." Times are changing!

But ye shall receive power, after that the Holy Ghost is come upon you: and ye shall be witnesses unto me (Acts 1:8 KJV).

BROTHER NOT A CHRISTIAN

I know that you must be right about praising God for everything. However, there is one thing that I am not able to praise God for. My brother is not a Christian and does not want to be. How can I thank God for this?

My Comments

You have two choices: you can thank God that your brother is not a Christian and does not want to be, or you can thank God that he is *going to be* a Christian. If you have asked God to bring your brother to Christ, your opportunity now is to *think of him* as coming to Christ. Think of him as already belonging to God. To me, this is a much better answer, and I believe it is the truth about praising God. Those who keep their eyes on what is bad, often live in fear. Those who place their confidence and trust in the promises Jesus gave, have a right to believe that God is answering their prayers.

This is the assurance we have in approaching God: that if we ask anything according to His will, He hears us. And if we know that He hears us - whatever we ask - we know that we have what we asked of Him (I John 5:14-15 NIV).

I HAVE DEMONS

My sister and brother-in-law are wonderful Spirit-filled Christians. My brother-in-law went to a seminar where there were Christian speakers. He called and told us about a class he attended on demonology.

The next day I prayed for my own deliverance from demons. I had no idea what to expect, but two demons left me. I asked my brother-in-law if he would pray for more demons to come out. We had listened to the tapes he had brought home, and I knew there were many demons in me. He held a regular deliverance service, and many demons fled. But I knew all of them had gone, for they talked to him (through me) and told him they were many.

I have the names of two more demons in me - numerology and mistakes. I know Satan is at work in me. How else can one person make so many mistakes? I have praised the Lord for my mistakes, but how long does He take to help us? I feel so drained. After the last mistake, I just don't know anymore.

My Comments

When our attention is centered in demons, demons can be seen in everything. I have seen Christian's get very happy when demons were thought to be cast out of them. But when these "delivered" persons had new problems they said, "I have another demon in me. Where can I find someone to cast it out?" This eventually leads to loss of faith, discouragement, and defeat.

Demon activity is real - let there be no doubt

of this. The disciples cast evil spirits out of people so they would be free to accept Jesus as their Savior. Then, with Christ within, they, too, had the authority to fight against Satan who was now on the outside. It is very important to recognize where Jesus is and where Satan is. Any misconception fills men with fear and eventually with doubt, even of their own salvation.

Greater is He that is in you (Jesus) than he (Satan) that is in the world (I John 4:4 KJV).

A DOUBTING THOMAS

Praise the Lord for people like you! Several weeks ago I was stricken with a severe allergic reaction to a medication for a strep infection. I was hospitalized because my legs were so inflamed I couldn't walk. After nine days, there was no improvement - in fact, I was getting worse. The doctor arrived Saturday afternoon and told me they could try another type of medication. If that didn't work, they didn't know what they were going to do.

The new medication would be started at midnight. I was scared. But I had just finished reading *Prison to Praise*, so I laid back on my pillow and in my own simple way gave myself over to the Lord. I kept telling Him how much I trusted Him.

Within fifteen minutes, all the swelling and pain had left, and I started walking! I felt a peacefulness I have never known. This was even before the new medicine was even started!

I have friends who tried to explain to me how easy it is to give one's life over to the Lord, but I was a doubting Thomas. I felt I had to know so much more and study so much more before I would be ready. But without my realizing what was happening, the Lord made it so easy for me.

My stay in the hospital was the greatest gift our Lord could have given me. He knows what He is doing. I am now reading your third book and can't put it down. Many of my friends are going to receive your books for Christmas. God love you and take care of you every minute of your life!

My Comments

Many complicated, involved solutions to healing, are advocated by well-meaning people (and some not so well-meaning). Healing comes by faith in God, as revealed through Christ.

If you are tempted to declare, "I have believed, but God has not done His part," please read the next paragraph carefully.

To have the faith Jesus taught, is easy, but

we make it complicated. If we admit that we are at fault, and never God, we open the door for the Holy Spirit to bring healing. If healing does not come instantly, do not cry, "It doesn't work." Say, "God is healing me." If anyone asks you, "How are you?" declare to them, "Wonderful!" Why say this? If we believe in our hearts that God is healing us, then we have the right and the responsibility to rejoice in that healing.

If thou shalt confess with thy mouth...and... believe in thine heart...thou shalt be saved (Romans 10:9 KJV).

The English word *saved*, is sozo in Greek. Strong's Concordance tells us that sozo means: to save, deliver, protect, to *heal*, preserve, and to be made whole.

BRAIN SURGERY

I read *Prison to Praise* in April of this year. I was scheduled for brain surgery to relieve the involuntary movement in my left side.

I have had cerebral palsy ever since I had a whooping cough shot. I read your book the day before I went into surgery. After surgery I had so much pain in my head I thought I was going to die! When my headache was so bad that I thought I couldn't stand it, I'd praise God for my pain. It would go away just like that! The minute I'd start feeling sorry for myself and say, "Oh, God, why are you letting this happen to me?" the pain would come back even worse than it was before!

The Lord has been so good to me. As I write this, I am filled with peace and completely without pain.

My Comments

"Sorry for myself" - a common failure! Self pity(or a grumbling attitude) holds back healing. This beautiful example of how God works should stimulate every reader's faith. In this case, the pain was so intense that God brought instant deliverance when this young lady praised Him. Often, pain has to flee when we praise God for the pain as it is. In other situations, He brings peace that enables us to rejoice in His love, and joy that overcomes the pain.

But He was wounded for our transgressions, He was bruised for our guilt and iniquities; the chastisement needful to obtain peace and well being for us was upon Him, and with the stripes that wounded Him we are healed and made whole (Isaiah 53:5 AMP).

A BLIND GIRL VISITS ME

One Saturday evening about ten o'clock, I received a telephone call asking me if I could talk to a girl who was nearly blind and desperately needed encouragement. The caller suggested that the girl probably would kill herself before morning unless someone helped her. I said that I would talk with her, although my natural inclination was to say that I couldn't at that late hour.

After the telephone conversation, I confess that a grumbling spirit tried to control my mind. I thought of the four services I would have the next day, how late it was, and about the prospect of receiving people that night at eleven o'clock. I also thought about the early hour I would be compelled to get up Monday morning to fly from California to Florida.

"Oh, Lord, will I have the strength to do all of this?" The Spirit said, "If you will praise Me and thank Me, you will experience something wonderful from this."

I couldn't think of anything wonderful that might happen, but I determined to be thankful for this late caller.

The people did not arrive until about 11:30 pm. I led the girl into our living room, while observing that she could see large objects. After sharing my faith in God's power to heal her, I felt urged to place my hands on her head and pray.

When I was through praying, I was directed to make a bold step of faith. I said, "Now open your eyes and tell me what you see."

"I see you in front of me." I opened my Bible and held it in front of the girl. She read from a fine-print Bible, word for word, and I knew that God had touched her eyes.

If I had permitted a spirit of grumbling to overwhelm my spirit of praise and thanksgiving, I would have prevented God from doing what He wanted to do.

There will be instances in your life in which God can powerfully change many situations if you faithfully practice thanking Him for everything. We never know what God will do until we follow His Word and thank Him in all situations.

Thank God in everything - no matter what the circumstances may be, be thankful and give thanks; for this is the will of God for you who are in Christ Jesus (I Thessalonians 5:18 AMP).

WHAT SHOULD I EAT

How can I praise the Lord when everything I eat causes me intense pain? The doctors cannot find anything wrong with me, but I keep on suffering. Should I stop eating? Should I lie and say I feel good when I don't?

My Comments

Many people carefully observe their body, and react to its slightest symptom. When the body says, "I feel good," they react in joy. When the body says, "I feel bad," they react in sadness or fear. Their body becomes the center of attention! It heaps demands upon demands. Anxious concentration is placed on "What should I eat? What should I not eat?"

When we give our bodies over to Him, they then become His responsibility! Matthew 6:25 says, *Do not worry about your life, what you will eat or drink.*

Once I had about 50 foods that made me ill. Now, almost nothing does. Satan learned that every time he used food to distress me, I praised the Lord for the distress! This cleared the way for God to heal me!

So whether you eat or drink or whatever you do, do it all for the glory of God (I Corinthians 10:31 NIV).

SEVEN CHRISTIAN FRIENDS

I do not know how to thank you enough for your prayers. I wrote and asked you to pray that God would help me to find some Christian fellowship here in prison. You wrote and told me that God would soon supply me with seven Christian friends. It was difficult for me to believe this, for there seemed to be no Christian men here. But you were right, and God has answered your prayers. I soon had seven Christian friends, and now the number has grown. I rejoice and praise the Lord for the wonderful things He is doing. Please send me six copies of *Prison to Praise*. There are men here who need to read it.

It is nearly unbelievable to see what God is doing. Thank you for sending us the first copies of *Prison to Praise*, for they have changed my life, and now the lives of many men.

My Comments

God is reaching into all levels of society and drawing members of His Body together. We can not even imagine the many ways that God will use us if we let the Holy Spirit lead us.

As you read this, ask God to lead you into whatever ministry He has designed for you. If His answer does not seem glamorous or exciting, do not refuse to listen! God has His plan, and although your part may seem small and unimportant, your obedience will bring tremendous results.

For He is our peace, Who has made us both one, and has broken down the dividing wall of hostility (Ephesians 2:14 RSV).

FROM A NUN

I can't thank you enough for the copies of *Prison to Praise* you sent to me. I will give them to those in need. Thanks to you, I am happy, and at peace. You helped me find the real Christ.

My Comments

What kind of faith have you found? Religion may give a sense of peace, because it satisfies our need to "do good." But religion doesn't give Christ's joy. One of Jesus' missions was to bring to us the secret of how to have joy: the fruit of His Holy Spirit is joy.

Rejoice that you were born in a country where you heard the Good News of what Jesus Christ came to the world to do. Rejoice in every detail of your life. Rejoice even when you do not know what to rejoice about!

You will show me the path of life; in Your presence is fullness of joy (Psalm 16:11 NKJV).

TWO WAYWARD SONS

I have been reading your books and have been trying to believe that something good is going to happen to my two sons. I raised them to believe in God and have taken them to church since they were babies. They refused to accept Christ, and have left home. I do not know where they are or what they are doing. How can I be thankful that they may be doing something wrong or may even be in jail, or a hospital? I would appreciate any help you can give me.

My Answer

Before your sons left, did you ask God to do whatever was necessary to help them accept Christ? If you did, are you willing to let God win them His way? Or will you insist that He do it your way? If you are willing to let God win your boys to Christ in His own way, He will answer your prayers. God is bound by His own promises to you, but He can do only what you trust Him to do.

I recommend that you believe God is using the present position of your boys to lead them to

Christ. Turn them over to Him and believe that He is carefully doing all that is necessary. They may need to go through difficult experiences. But that will be far better than having no problems and dying without knowing Jesus as Savior.

I will say to the North, 'Give them up!' and to the South, 'Do not hold them back!' Bring my sons from afar and my daughters from the ends of the earth (Isaiah 43:6 NIV).

FROM A JEWISH GIRL

I am so glad God led me to purchase *Prison to Praise.*

My mother has never confessed Christ as Messiah and Savior. This bothered me continually. Satan had a field day until you taught me to trust God. I am now at peace concerning Mom (and all my family), knowing He does inhabit the praises of His people.

My Comments

Christians all too often live in torment over the spiritual condition of their loved ones. They feel it would be wrong for them to carry anything less than a heavy burden for those they love.

This is one of Satan's most clever tricks. He uses our "burden" to rob us of Christ's joy. If we are overflowing with thanksgiving and praise, God uses our praise to increase our faith! And our faith releases God's power to work in our loved ones.

Jesus gained the victory for us! We are to rejoice in what He is doing for those we love. If this Jewish girl can believe for her family, you and I can too!

Thou art holy, enthroned on the praises of Israel (Psalm 22:3 RSV).

I REFUSED

The Lord called me to serve Him, forty years ago, but I refused. Many people could have been helped if I had not decided to do just what I wanted to do. I cannot see any reason to thank God that I turned Him down. It bothers me every time I think about it. Can you help me?

My Comments

If we dwell on our mistakes, they will continue to hurt us, and the blessing we could now be to the world will never happen. But if we thank God, He will take our mistakes, and use them to help others. Give thanks that He is doing it, and He *will*. He promises to!

I knew a man in this same situation who turned his problem over to God, and was quickly filled with an amazing joy. When he spoke to young people about the mistakes he had made in choosing his life's work, they responded. Many of these young people have now gone into full-time Christian work, as a result of this man's faith that God would use even his past mistakes.

In this man's case, it is easy to see the benefits of praising God for ourselves, as we are, but in others it is not so evident. However, it is not our job to see the evidence! Our responsibility is to believe that God will take our life, as it is, and use everything we have done, or not done, to build His Kingdom. If you want to waste the rest of your life feeling sorry about your mistakes, that is your choice. But I can tell you that it does not have to be that way! Praise Him for your mistakes, believe that He has been and will continue working them for your good, and you will experience new joy and strength.

The joy of the Lord is your strength (Nehemiah 8:10 NIV).

———————————

PRAISE AND THANKS

It may seem an unimportant question, but I want to know the difference between praise and thanks. Or is there a difference?

My Comments

Ephesians 5:20 reads: *Giving thanks always for all things unto God and the Father in the name of our Lord Jesus Christ* (KJV). In Strong's Concordance, the Greek words that are translated *giving thanks* mean: To be grateful, to express gratitude.

According to Strong's Concordance, to praise God means to applaud, to celebrate, to glory in, and to honor. The sacrifice of praise in Hebrews 13:15 means an offering of thanksgiving or praise.

How do we apply this in our lives? To give thanks to God and to praise the Lord is to say, "Lord, I don't understand how you can bring anything good out of this, but I'm trusting your loving wisdom." It is saying, "I'm really hurting, Lord, but I'm casting all my hurts and cares on you. And, by the way Lord, I'm casting myself on your great mercy. I trust you, Lord, and I trust your infinite love for me."

Praise our God, 0 peoples, let the sound of His praise be heard (Psalm 66:8 NIV).

BE THANKFUL AND STILL ASK

How can I be thankful for my life as it is, and still ask God to change things? I don't understand.

My Comments

When we ask God to change anything it is most important that our attitude be pleasing to Him.

Consider the case of the Jews in the desert. It was hot and dusty and they were carrying all their possessions. For three days they had no water. Their bodies were craving liquid. It would have been natural for them to plead with God for help. But they chose to complain!

Their attitude was wrong. They didn't see God as the One who loved them and wanted to supply their needs. They felt He was failing them.

Their attitude caused God to be angry. He declared that all the complainers would never enter the Promised Land.

This story reveals how much God hates complaining. He wants us to pray and to ask Him to meet all our needs. But He wants our prayers to be based on trust in His wisdom, His love and His perfect justice.

If the Jews had said, "God, You have us here in the desert for our own good. We disobeyed You and now we are suffering the consequences. We will stay here in the desert until You decide to lead us out. We are thirsty because we need to be - to teach us obedience. But, Father, we are weak and desperate. We plead for your mercy. Please give us water!" The history of their journey would have been different. God would have given them water and probably led them out of the desert much sooner.

We should come to God with a thankful heart. "You know what is best for me, Father. You are working good in my life. I love and trust You. But, Father, I hurt. Please reach out and touch me. Please help me to believe all your promises."

Blessed be the Lord, who daily loads us with benefits (Psalm 68:19 NKJV).

GOD BLESSED MY SON

My son was an excellent example of a good boy. He has been a fine Christian in every sense of the word. He is a loving husband and a real father to his own children. His church and community respect him.

Some time back his job fell apart. The company that employed him lost business, and his pay kept falling. When he was down to working two days a week, he had to sell his beautiful home. He kept believing God would help him.

My son used the equity from the sale of his home to purchase a business. We all prayed and believed that this was the reason his job had become so poor. We praised the Lord for giving him this new very prosperous-looking business opportunity.

But the business venture collapsed, and our faith was at a low ebb. Then we found *Prison to Praise* in our local bookstore. We united in thanking God for the whole thing just as it was.

A completely unexpected thing happened - something we had never dreamed of. God spoke to my son and told him he was to enter full-time Christian work. The guidance was clear and positive. Finally, our eyes were open and we saw what God wanted to do. Now we are rejoicing! We have learned to trust Him in a new way.

My Comments

When we thank and praise God for devastating problems, we open the way for Him to make things work for our good. He can even use our failures. He wants us to rejoice in His answers, before we see them.

Trust in the Lord with all your heart and lean not on your own understanding; In all your ways acknowledge Him and He will make your paths straight (Proverbs 3:5-6 NIV).

I RESENTED MY WEAKNESS

For more years than I can remember, I resented my physical weakness. I thought of how many things I could do for God if I didn't become exhausted so easily.

I knew something was causing my weakness, and I prayed daily to be healed. I tried to believe that God healed me through Christ, but the physical weakness continued, and grew worse with age.

Then I read *Prison to Praise*. It seemed ridiculous to be thankful for my weakness, but I tried.

Then my praise started taking effect. I soon believed that God could use me exactly as I was. A new joy over, "me as I was," grew inside. I learned to like the "me" that I was. With this came a gradual, yet obvious, change in my body. I felt less and less tired. I keep getting stronger!

Praise the Lord for what has happened to me.

My Comments

God wanted this lady to praise Him so He could manifest His strength in her weakness. If you have a physical, emotional, or mental weakness, praise God for "you" just as you are. He will take your praise and lift you to new heights, in whatever way He selects. If you expect Him to do for you exactly what He has done for someone else, you may be disappointed. Trust God to do for you what He knows is best, and I promise you, you will always be thoroughly and completely satisfied!

As thy days, so shall thy strength be (Deuteronomy 33:25 KJV).

I DIDN'T MEAN IT

I prayed, "God I believe You, and I will trust You to work this thing out for good." But I didn't mean it. I didn't believe God would work it out. And the situation keeps getting worse. No matter how I pray, it gets more painful. If I tell God that I believe He will work this thing out for my good, it is just plain lying. What do I do?

My Comments

We must be honest with God, and say, "I want to trust You, but I can't believe that You are going to change this terrible situation. Please help me! Jesus, help me believe." It is good to find a scripture promise that addresses our particular need, such as Jeremiah 29:11 which says: *For I know the plans I have for you...plans to prosper you...plans to give you hope and a future.*

Then we can honestly say, "Jesus is helping me to believe God's promises. With His help I can grow in trusting God."

To admit that we cannot believe God without His help, is a greater blessing than to think we can have faith without His help!

Lord, I believe; help thou mine unbelief (Mark 9:24 KJV).

EPILEPSY

I had epileptic seizures every week of my life. Only those who have lived with this disease know the horror it brings. After I knew Jesus as my Savior, I was less unhappy, but the seizures continued. When I heard about praising the Lord *for* my sickness, it sure didn't make any sense to me. How could I, a young person, be thankful for this horrible thing?

But as I praised the Lord, my faith grew. The

seizures decreased in frequency and intensity. Jesus was healing me. I stopped taking my medicine and still felt well. When my parents found out about the medicine, they were upset and wanted me to go back on it. I begged them to let me continue as I was. They insisted that I had to go to the doctor to see what he said.

I was given a brain-wave test and fully expected the results to be negative. The doctor surprised me when he said there was still positive evidence that my brain was suffering from epilepsy, and that I had to go back on my medication. I said, "But why haven't I had any seizures for several months if I am still so ill?" He had no explanation for this, but said I was sure to have continued attacks.

I was confused. What should I do? My parents were now even more insistent that I go back to my medicine. In prayer, I felt a returning peace, and a certainty that God was healing me. I again begged my parents to let me stay off the medicine until they saw the first positive evidence that I had to have it. To this, they finally agreed.

This was over a year ago! I have taken no medicine and have enjoyed perfect health. I thank the Lord for teaching me to praise Him, and trust Him. Your books on praise have greatly fortified my faith, and I thank you for helping me to enjoy the great blessing of health.

My Comment

Very often I am asked, "Should I stop taking my medicine if I am believing God to heal me?" I always say, "Let the Holy Spirit guide you. Only He knows how God wants to heal you." Those who say, "You should throw away your medicine," are wrong. This advice, to those who do not have the faith for healing, can bring unnecessary pain and suffering. When the Holy Spirit gives us the faith to know that we are healed, that is the time to stop taking medicine.

But He was pierced for our transgressions, He was crushed for our iniquities; the punishment that brought us peace was upon Him, and by His wounds we are healed (Isaiah 53:5 NIV).

A CATHOLIC SISTER WRITES TO OTHER CATHOLIC SISTERS

I have some good news to share with you. For thirty years my full-time work has been teaching people how to get to heaven. A few weeks ago I found out how easy it is!

I was talking to Sister Rose, and she showed me a book called *Prison to Praise*. She gave me all kinds of reasons why I should read it. While she was trying to convince me, I was thinking about all the work I had to do in my office; the things I had to prepare for my first communion class; and besides all that, I was supposed to help with the spring housecleaning here at the convent. However, I took the book - just to be polite. The next day I decided I better read a few pages, just so I could tell Sister Rose I had started it. I found it so exciting I could not put it down.

The author, Merlin Carothers, was in the Army, and he was also in prison. I won't tell you about the crimes he committed. He was an intelligent man and the FBI had a hard time catching him. When he got out of prison, he was almost a millionaire, and still a young man. He made his money in a dishonest way, but the FBI had not found out about that.

Mr. Carothers made the mistake of going to visit his grandmother on a Sunday afternoon. She wanted him to go to church with her that evening. He said he couldn't go because one of his friends was coming to pick him up. This was a big lie. He tried to call all of his friends to ask someone to pick him up, but nobody answered, so he had to go to church with his grandmother. He thought, *What a foolish way to spend a Sunday evening when there are so many exciting things to do.*

At church, he noticed how happy the people were - much happier than he was, in spite of his money. That night God changed his life. God filled this criminal with His grace and love. Later he became an Army chaplain, and went back to the very same place he had been a handcuffed prisoner.

Chaplain Carothers found out that the most powerful prayers are prayers of praise and thanksgiving. (Most of us are always saying prayers of "Give me this" or "Give me that.") He studied the Bible and realized that God, the most loving of Fathers, has planned every detail of our lives with the most loving care. The chaplain tells about many people who came to him for advice. He told them that God had permitted their problems, and that He would bring good out of them, if they would praise and thank Him. Naturally, he had great difficulty convincing most people that this was true, but once they praised and thanked God for their problems, great things did happen!

All types of people came to the chaplain: some were very sick, others were in deep depression, some on the verge of committing suicide. He told them God loves them, and God would bring good out of these things if they would praise and thank Him for them. Many of these people said, "But I have never done very much for God. I really don't deserve to have God do anything for me. He told them that was true. None of us deserve to receive God's gifts, but God does not give us His gifts because we deserve them. He gives His gifts because He loves us. All we have to do is to believe that He loves us.

It is easy to trust God when everything is going fine. It is difficult when we have a serious illness, are in a car accident, or out of work, etc. God tells us that He has permitted these things, and that if we trust Him, He will bring good out of them.

It makes me very sad when I meet so many people who think it is hard to get to heaven. These people travel the road of fear, when they should travel the road of love. When we realize that God loves us, we must love Him. God's love is a million times greater than the love of any mother for her child.

These books filled me with such joy and peace, I had to tell you about them. There is only one difficulty about reading these books: most people who read them want to buy one for each of their friends, and this could be expensive.

I hope I have convinced you that you should read these books, but just in case I haven't, I dare you to read them. I guarantee you that you will be amazed at the happy results.

My Comments

With publicity like this, the praise books will reach into the farthest corners of the world! Thank you, Sister, for believing enough to do something to share your belief with others.

There is no greater stimulus to our own enthusiasm than to share it with others. God does not give us His blessings to keep to ourselves. Rather, Jesus told us to go tell the good news of the Gospel to all people.

Neither do men light a candle, and put it under a bushel, but on a candlestick; and it giveth light unto all that are in the house (Matthew 5:15 KJV).

TRY HARDER - MORE TROUBLE

We desperately need your prayers. We have so many problems, I don't even know where to begin.

My husband drinks all the time. For fifteen years he drank a lot, but now it is all the time that he is off work. He loves his drinking friends, but has no time for his family. He thinks his friends are perfect, and there is nothing good about us. His hatred caused our very young daughter to get pregnant by a boy of another color. The boy wants to marry her, but my husband will not allow it.

You wouldn't believe how often my husband has beaten me. This only happens when he is drunk, but since he is drunk all the time, I live in fear. I have tried with all my heart to be a good wife! but nothing I do is right. I want us to go to church and have a Christian family, but he won't go.

When he beats me, he is usually sorry the next day and tells me he will never do it again. Then he acts as if he loves me, and I know I do love him. Despite what he does, I love him. It breaks my heart to see our lives and family thrown away.

I got away from the God I knew when I was a young girl, but I know He is still there. The harder I try to get close to Him, the more troubles we have. Please tell me what to do.

My Comments

This problem is different from the ones many people have, but the cause is the same. Sometimes it is difficult to see why people have to go through such frustration. In this situation, it is easier to see what is happening. She writes, "The harder I try to get closer to Him, the more troubles we have." When anyone tries to get closer to God, Satan will rear his ugly head.

He attacks those who want to get close to God. The weapon she uses are many, but the plan is the same. If he can keep our eyes on our problems, he can keep our eyes off God! But we can turn the tables on him by thanking God for whatever is happening.

She is getting close enough to God to give Satan cause to worry. It may hurt to think of Satan using someone we love to fight against us, but remember that Satan will use anyone who will let him. Whether she chooses to stay with her husband and seek help, or leave him, she should know that God loves her and will use her situation to help her. Her faith in God will release God's power to help her entire family.

You have caused men to ride over our heads; We went through fire and through water; but You brought us out to rich fulfillment (Psalm 66:12 NKJV).

FOR OTHERS

I have heard several authors speak, and they were just plain blah. From beginning to end, I didn't know what they were talking about.

When I went with my parents to hear you, I wasn't looking forward to it. "Another writer?"

I wailed.

I tried to get set as comfortable as possible to endure whatever of your ideas you might be expounding on. But when you opened your mouth, you immediately got my attention. I could see you really believed in what you were saying. I relaxed and decided to listen for at least a little while.

The longer you talked, the more interested I got. You seemed so happy, I started feeling happy myself. I realized I was sitting on the edge of the pew trying not to miss a word. Your ideas on praising God were unique, but you sort of pulled me in. As you poured out one illustration after another about the power of praise, I became even more interested. Your enthusiasm and excitement were really catching!

I didn't have any real big problems in my own life, but I thought of what your ideas could do to help other people. I've always wanted to do something to help other people, but I had never thought of anything that I could do.

By the end of your message, I was really high. I could see that most of the people were excited, too. Even then I was amazed at the number of people who went forward when you gave an invitation. Most of them were weeping, and I've never seen anything like that in my church.

But what happened that night isn't the

reason I'm writing. When I went back to college the next day, I decided I was going to put your ideas into practice. When anything happened that seemed a little unpleasant, I said aloud, "Praise the Lord" (but usually not very loud). It worked! I kept feeling better all day. I was excited over my discovery.

The next day I started saying, "Praise the Lord," loud enough for other people to hear it. They usually laughed at me, but I noticed that when they mimicked me, they had smiles on their faces. Several of them said, "Praise the Lord" to me when we passed in the halls. I knew they were sort of making fun of me, but I also saw we were becoming better friends. Then some of these same kids wanted to talk with me about "this new kick I was on." When I explained, they were not convinced, but I asked them to try it. Several have already told me they are now much happier. Some of them haven't accepted Christ yet, but the door is opening, and I'm at last getting the chance to do something for others.

My Comments

To do something for others - this is a powerful need in every Christian's heart. We feel the desire but often don't know what to do. Here is something you can "get your teeth into," Every time something unpleasant happens to you, say, "Praise the Lord." Try it when you are alone first, then let others in on your secret. Instead of your usual grumble, when you have to do something you prefer not to do, give a hearty "Praise the Lord."

You may not feel like praising the Lord, but do it anyhow. (God won't hold back the blessing because you don't feel like it.) When others see and hear your happy responses, they will be drawn to respond as you do. God will bless them and you!

Do not let any unwholesome talk come out of your mouths, but only what is helpful for building others up according to their needs, that it may benefit those who listen (Ephesians 4:29 NIV).

DISC JOCKEY

Prison to Praise introduced us to praising God for all things. My husband and I believed that all things work together for our good. We thought Christians should praise God *in* all circumstances, but praising God *for* all circumstances was a new idea to us. At the time we were having difficulties with our rebellious fifteen-year-old son, and we praised the Lord for each manifestation of his rebellion.

As things got progressively worse, with each day bringing a major crisis, we gave up in despair and placed our son in a treatment center. At this point we reread *Prison to Praise* and *Power in Praise*. Convinced that this was the only pathway to victorious living, we began again to thank God for our son exactly as he was. Again the crises came thick and fast.

On a Friday night, we faced a particularly hard praise challenge and called my sister to join us in a little prayer chapel to praise and pray. We left there with some measure of peace and a determination to continue to praise, but still no real joy.

The next morning, I was home alone when the phone rang. It was a disc jockey on the local "rock" radio station. He offered me the money in their cash jackpot if I could tell him the exact amount of money in it. I told him my two teenagers were gone, that by choice I never listened to his station and had no idea how much money was in his pot. He told me I had just lost $1,057.55.

I hung up the phone and praised the Lord for the loss of $1,057.55. The more I praised the Lord, the more genuine my praise became; the more I thought about what would have happened had the kids been home to answer the phone, the more jubilant I became.

By the time my husband came home, an hour and a half later, I was skipping through the house. I told him what had happened. It took a minute for him to get on my wave length. Our expenses with psychiatrists, psychologists, etc., for our son, had been astronomical, and $1,057.55 did sound pretty good. But soon he began to praise, too.

That was the first time a radio station had called us, and the first time we had an opportunity to win money. Just as my husband said, "Well,if the Lord had wanted you to have it, you would have known the amount," the phone rang. When my husband answered, he turned to me and asked, "How much was it that we didn't win?" I said, "$1,057.55," and he repeated it into the phone. Then he came back and sat down.

"We just won $1,057.55," he said.

"We what?"

"Yes. It was the same radio station with another disc jockey calling."

Two calls in one day when we had never had one such call in our entire lives. It was His sweet assurance that our praise pleased Him. It bolstered our faith in the power of praise!

I would like to report that we have not wavered since then, but the going is still rough. We know He is working things out perfectly, but we know it only by faith, and our praise is still sometimes tearful.

My Comments

One day we will realize that God has His own plan, and does His work in the way He wants to do it. Please do not read the above letter and think, "I wish God would give me $1,000 to meet my needs." Thank Him that He is meeting your needs in just the right way. He knows exactly what is best for the eternal spirit that lives within you.

Please, do not misunderstand me. I'm not saying that God wants anyone to be poor. Many people are poor because they have been unwise. I am saying that if you have done your very best to claim God's promises of prosperity, and are still poor, you may well need to ask yourself: Am I being wise in how I handle the money that I do have? Am I honoring God with my finances? If your answer is yes to both of these questions, then you can trust that God is providing what you need. Rejoice and be glad in it. Your praise may release your need, and God will then prosper you!

Honor the Lord with your capital and sufficiency from righteous labors, and with the first fruits of all your income (Proverbs 3:9 AMP).

———————————

PRAISE POWER

It was a real blessing to read *Answers to Praise*, apparently hot off the press. How it must thrill you from the tip of your toes to the top of your head to see the way God is using you!

It would take about 100 typewritten pages to cover the past year, but I'm condensing this testimony into a few basics. It is exciting to see the miracle God did, and how it has affected lives around me.

For many years, I attended church, but there was always a wall between God and me - a wall I was afraid to break. Then, three years ago our Methodist church planned a lay-witness mission. I managed to get involved in the planning, much to my dismay. I knew that during the mission I would make a commitment to God and that frightened me.

During the meetings, all the outsiders kept saying, "God loves you, and I love you." I felt terribly uncomfortable. During the final Sunday's message, I felt like the coordinator was looking straight through me. He had an altar call for those who wanted more of God in their lives - or something on that order. I found myself going forward, as if a magnet was drawing me. I didn't understand then that, according to Scripture, the Holy Spirit draws men to Christ. I'd never read the Bible. But the shell was broken, and I was open to learn.

About this time, our son became desperately ill with a paralytic disease. I spent hours weeping and sobbing, feeling that my world had caved in. Oh, that someone had told me about Christ and the victorious life we can live in Him through praise!

My mom arranged for us to visit a faith healer, a spiritualist. I didn't realize the dangers involved. After working with our son for a time, the healer had him walking across a room, the first steps in many months. She saw him a second time, and this time he felt electricity going through his body. But when we got back home, our son could not even crawl on his belly. He kept regressing until the paralysis affected his hands and even his optical nerves. I was desperate for help and thoroughly confused.

Next, I visited the Science of Mind church, knowing that several friends were quite happy there. I returned home with a book on "ultimate reality" - and all sorts of inner confusion and turmoil. I began to wonder who Jesus was, whether he was just a man, and I even began to wonder if God was real. Finally, I literally sobbed out, "God - if You are - I'm all confused and mixed up, and I don't know where to go or what to believe. Help me. Who is Jesus? Is He really God? I've got to know. Oh, help me." Boy! I didn't realize what I was asking for. Things began to happen. Fast.

At a luncheon, I heard about Jesus in a new way. A young couple giving their testimony really touched my heart, and I noticed the next day in church that I felt strangely exuberant.

After church I was at home in the bathroom just singing away, and I found myself singing out in funny sounds; almost like an opera. I was dumbfounded. Later, I was engrossed in a book on spiritual healing. As I read accounts of healings, I had a funny sensation. Words in a funny language poured out of my mouth! I wondered what on earth was happening to me. Fortunately (God always arranges things so nicely!) I had the phone number of the luncheon leader. I contacted her and found out I probably had received the Baptism in the Holy Spirit. She thought I must be speaking in tongues, but I had never heard of such a thing. I didn't realize, of course, that speaking in tongues brings edification and power.

Two weeks after this experience, my son was re-hospitalized 150 miles away from home. I tried to keep my chin up, but found myself dreadfully depressed and downtrodden. With three other handicapped children at home to care for, I became so exhausted, I could barely function. I thought of running away and never coming back. But I continued to attend the luncheons, which uplifted me a bit. Then it happened.

My friend invited me to a New Year's Eve service at the Assembly. This was a foreign idea to me, attending church on New Year's Eve. But, no one had invited us to a party (Praise the Lord!) and I was in no shape to give one myself. So I dragged my husband along, and there we were, watching those funny people raise their hands in prayer. I thought, "Ye gads, what will my husband think of all this?" Then, I noticed he was playing follow the leader. I thought, "What the heck," lifted my own arms in praise, and the depression left like magic, never to return. I have been on cloud nine ever since, except short, intermittent periods, and they were my fault.

I learned that spiritism is of the devil and renounced all association with it. I began to realize that our son's false healing was Satanic. I praise God for opening my eyes to so much. I'd been taught that hell and Satan were not real. I learned the truth in those areas, too. The hospital allowed our son to come home on a visit. I arranged a genuine healing service at our church for him and for others in need. I honestly believed that our son would hop right out of his wheelchair and run down the aisles, but he didn't move a muscle. God had much more for us to learn.

The next evening, the evangelist asked if any who fasted and prayed for healings felt their prayers were not answered. Guess who jumped up. He had me place my hand on the Bible and claim God's healing promises. I fell prostrate for over an hour, and God spoke to me, saying, "He is healed." Praise God for the gift of faith, as I never again doubted the healing, though there was no visible evidence of it.

The hospital called me a few days later and chewed me out royally for taking my son out in public. Our paralyzed son, with little respiratory system left, was sick as a dog, running a high fever. I knew this was Satanic and rebuked Satan in the name of Jesus and told him to get lost. "God tells me my son is healed, and I believe Him!" I said.

The next morning, our son could lift his legs, roll over in bed, and crawl on his hands and knees. He astonished everyone. The hospital staff looked for logical reasons for the overnight recovery. After three weeks, he experienced another setback and the hospital sent him home. For three weeks, I cared for a paralyzed boy whose wheelchair weighs sixty-five pounds. It was rough to keep praising God, but because I knew my son was healed I ignored the problem.

I didn't feel burdened.

Then sickness descended again. He caught the flu, but as we praised God, he improved rapidly. One day, he could partially dress himself; the next day he could climb into a tub, etc. This summer, he began walking a few steps. By August, he was riding a bike and climbing trees. He has everyone astounded! His wheelchair and all the trimmings have been donated to the school for handicapped children, as he can now climb right up the school bus steps without assistance. Praise God!

This is just one tiny portion of what God has done in my life the past few months. It is truly fantastic. I know no other word to describe all the emotional and physical healings we've experienced. I had asked God to reveal Himself to me. He continues to answer my prayer in mighty ways.

My Comments

Reading and answering piles of letters often exhausts me. I finished this letter with a song of joy and experienced new strength in my own body. Has this letter done anything for you? If you wrestle with the problem of physical healing, read the letter again. Ask the Holy Spirit to help you understand how God worked.

Let us hold unswervingly to the hope we profess, for He who promised is faithful (Hebrews 10:23 NIV).

GUILTY FOR BECOMING SICK

Since Jesus became a living reality in my life, and I have been filled with His Holy Spirit, I accepted Him as my Healer. Previously I had the colds, headaches, and aches that most elderly people have. But I found a new health that gives my life a new kind of joy. I shared this experience with many of my Christian friends and helped them to have new health. Others didn't understand, but were thankful for what I had.

One morning I became violently ill, and my husband took me to the doctor. The doctor rushed me to the hospital. Several doctors dropped what they were doing and prepared to operate. Everything happened so quickly, I could hardly believe it was me. My husband agreed with the doctors that I should have surgery.

I was shocked. How could I be physically ill when Jesus had so clearly made me well? I had perfect peace that He would always supply all I needed. But I couldn't deny that I was violently ill and had signs of approaching death. I agreed to the operation. They found a malignant cancer that they believed would have killed me that very day.

When I recovered, and on the way back to health, my faith was in deep turmoil. Had I failed God? Would my friends' faith in God be shattered by my own failure? What should I tell them about an experience I didn't understand myself? I could find no rest, and no peace. I know I am God's child, but carry great guilt that I have failed Him so miserably.

My Comments

This kind of guilt and fear is growing in our Christian community. As God is bringing health and healing to many, others are falling into fear and condemnation. This fear is fed by those who declare it is wrong to accept illness. Those who (rightly) share God's healing power are sometimes unwise in not completing their ministry by sharing God's will for us to praise and thank Him. It is true that He does want us to be well, but it is also true that our spiritual weakness sometimes keeps Him from healing us. Should we then lament our weakness and groan because of our failure? I do not believe so. Every time we fail, we are a testimony to one all-important fact. We are imperfect, but Christ is perfect. We need Christ to supply what we are not. Our imperfection is a powerful reminder to us that we need Christ to supply what we cannot do or be. This is God's will. Paul received many powerful answers to prayer, yet he had to endure one thing that he had asked God to remove. This reminded him of his weakness, and kept him dependent upon Christ.

Of course, others may be wounded by our lack of perfect faith. That is not our problem; it is His. He has accepted us as His own and understands that there are many things that we do not understand.

We should not say, "I'll just accept all sickness that comes along," and not exert our faith to be well in Christ. We should reach out as far as we can, believe Him, and trust Him to take care of whatever problems develop.

Too many people are needlessly suffering with guilt. Guilt and condemnation never help faith to grow, but praise and thanksgiving will multiply our faith to receive the blessings that God has ready for us.

Do not let your hearts be troubled. Trust in God (John 14:1 NIV).

———————

IN RUSSIA

In 1968 I had the opportunity to go to Moscow, Russia, as a tourist. On the second day there, during a guided tour, I fell and badly sprained my ankle. The pain was so terrific that I nearly passed out. The guide called for medical assistance, and an ambulance arrived with men in white coats. Through the translator, they told me I had an exceptionally bad sprain, and shouldn't put any weight on my leg. They bandaged it, which seemed to make it hurt worse.

When the men finished, I asked them where I could get crutches. They didn't know. They didn't even know where a cane could be purchased or borrowed. A friend with me asked if an ice pack would help my ankle. They said it might. No one offered to help me, so I hobbled over to our car and returned to the hotel. With agonizing pain I managed to get to our room.

My friend went downstairs to try to locate some ice, and aspirin, or any pain killer. By this time, my leg was badly swollen. When I took the bandage off, I could see the entire ankle was black and blue. The pain was so bad, I had to do something to get my mind off it.

I thought of singing. The only song that came to my mind was "Praise God from Whom All Blessings Flow." Gritting my teeth, and singing, I did my best. By the end of the chorus, something strange had happened to the ankle. The pain was gone! I stood up and walked around and laughed and laughed. The ankle was still swollen and black, but there was absolutely no pain.

When my friend came back, she couldn't believe me when I told her the pain was gone. The next morning, the ankle was still black, but the swelling had started to go down. Still no pain! No trace of pain ever came back to the ankle. I hadn't read *Prison to Praise* then and didn't know about the powerful force of praise, but now I understand why God touched me.

My Comment

What a powerful commentary on the power of praise! God used praise to bring healing although this woman only intended to get her mind off her pain. What healing could be released in this world if we would praise Him continually!

The reservoir of power within you may be dormant, but your praise and trust in God could release healing and life to many, many people. God will use your praise to set many captives free!

I will sing praise to the Name of the Lord Most High (Psalm 7:17 NKJV).

———————————

ASK GOD FOR MERCY

Only God knows what I have suffered - lung trouble, stomach trouble, heart trouble, severe dizziness, depression, weakness, and fear. Would you ask God to have mercy on me and heal me and take away this terrible fear? I was very sick all summer with high blood pressure. My husband doesn't seem to want to help me.

I think all this trouble is the result of almost a lifetime of brooding over my husband's interest in other women. I also have a low blood sugar condition. I am forty-eight years old, and with all my sickness I don't know if I can carry on.

My Comments

God has not caused this woman's problems. Satan has brought this sickness, fear, and depression upon her. God gave His only Son to die for this woman, in order to provide her with peace of mind and physical healing along with forgiveness of her sins (Isaiah 53:5). Like many people, she is brooding over problems while asking God to solve them. God has already made provision for each of our needs. Jesus accepted our sickness, sins and distresses on the Cross. His part is complete! Oh, if people could only see this! God wants us to believe that through Jesus He meets all our needs (Philippians 4:19).

How can this dear woman be set free? By thanking God for her husband, just as he is, and for herself, just as she is. When she rejoices that God is working out His perfect plan, she will then be at peace. Her physical problems will be as nothing compared to the peace she experiences. I believe this can usher her into better health. It probably will not be instantaneous, but will gradually make a big change in the self-pity and anxiety she has labored under for so long.

Our greatest need is to realize that God has already met all our needs through His Son. Our part is to accept His gift. Of course, it isn't an easy thing for us to do. But we can start by accepting our lives, exactly as they are, and believe that God is working out His perfect plan for us. He is!

God has not given us a spirit of fear, but of power, and of love and of a sound mind (II Timothy 1:7 NKJV).

I FEEL LIKE WALKING PAIN

Writing this is so painful. Two weeks ago, my beautiful seventeen-year-old son ran out the door, in below-zero weather, wearing only his under-shorts and socks - hallucinating from a huge amount of LSD. He was found frozen to death. I am trying to praise God. I praised Him while the whole town was searching for our son and while he was dying. Now I don't know. Please tell me specifically how to praise God.

I feel so guilty. We failed our son in a million ways - when he needed us most. I know God forgives me, but I am having so much trouble forgiving myself. I feel like walking pain.

My Answer

The boy who ran out of the house was not controlled by his own mind. A drug had taken over. He was not even aware of what he was doing.

The lasting results of your son's death now depend on you. Of course, Satan meant it to destroy you, your faith, and your family. But by offering the sacrifice of praise, you can now defeat him. What Satan meant for evil, God can use to bring forth good.

Believe that God will use the entire incident to work out good! He used the senseless death of Jesus on the Cross, and He can use your son's death to bring light and hope to others. How? Through your faith, His power is released. He will use everything for good *if* you trust Him.

Your son's death could profit nothing, if nothing is done to make it do so. Fear, anguish, self-pity, regrets, guilt, doubts - all fall right into

Satan's plan. If you succumb to these things, you will be used, just as your son was used. His temptation was LSD. Yours is guilt and fear and pain. They kill and destroy just as LSD does. Guilt and self blame can make you as helpless to gain victory as your son was. God understands this, and He has provided praise, to release His mighty power to bring something glorious out of this tragedy. *He* will - not you!

Trust in the Lord with all your heart and lean not on your own understanding (Proverbs 3:5 NKJV).

I WAS SHOT

A young woman said to me at the close of a meeting, "A girl friend of mine received a copy of *Prison to Praise* from a friend who had received it from another friend. Your book changed my life. I tried to get my husband to read it, but he refused. Then he was involved in an accident where he was shot with a gun four times."

She introduced me to her husband. He said, "I don't know why I wasn't interested in reading the book, but I just wasn't. After I was shot and was in the hospital, I had a little time to think. One bullet had gone through a lung. Another had torn away parts of six ribs. One went through my neck. I was really messed up. When my wife brought the book to me then, I agreed to read it. I was still very weak, as it had been only two days since the accident.

"As I read your book, I was absolutely amazed at the things God did in your life. By the end of it, I had started thanking Him that I had been shot. A voice inside me said, 'Okay you can stand up and walk now. You have learned what you needed to know.'

"I pulled the tubes and wires out of me and got up. When the nurses saw me, they started hollering, 'Get back in bed!'

'No, I can't,' I told them. 'God has made me well.'

"The doctors came and were so astonished they didn't know what to do. I was still very weak, but I got my clothes and went home. I had no pain and no problems from then on. Thank you for writing that book."

My Comments

Four couples who knew this man and his wife stood around them saying, "Isn't it wonderful! God did this for him," and "I saw him in the hospital before he read your book." Their beaming faces told me more than their words did.

Yes, it is wonderful. Wonderful is exactly

what God wants to do for people who have become bogged down in their problems. Problems are needed only until we learn what we need to know. We are then free to go on to more important things.

Many, O Lord my God, are Your wonderful works which You have done; And Your thoughts toward us...are more than can be numbered (Psalm 40:5 NKJV).

WE WERE HAPPY

My life and the lives of my little girls were shattered six weeks ago when my husband walked out on us for another woman. He has always lived an extremely moral and high-principled life, but has no religious beliefs at all. When anyone tries to witness to him, he strongly resents it. We've had a happy marriage, or at least I thought it was happy until this happened. The woman says she loves him and he loves her. He is going to file for divorce. We've had little things in our marriage that have always made it seem extra-special. We were both virgins when we became as one, and we've never even left one another for a brief errand without kissing each other good-bye.

The one major thing missing from our

marriage has been God. I was reared very religiously, but drifted away from God in my college years, and I could feel a void in my life, but didn't know exactly what it was. Since my husband has been gone, I have re-dedicated my life to God, and feel closer to Him than I have in a long time. Even with the closeness to God, though, I get so despondent and depressed that I've even thought of taking my life.

A friend of mine loaned me your book *Prison to Praise* and I received a great inspiration from it. Since then, I have been thanking God for my husband's leaving and even for this other woman, but I haven't been able to feel the joy and peacefulness that the Holy Spirit gives. I've committed this whole thing to God, and asked Him for my husband's salvation. My husband has always been such a good person, that he thinks he doesn't need God.

My Comments

When things are going well, we often do not realize our need of God. Our marriage and home may be holding together while we continue to do things we know we shouldn't, and leave undone things we know we should do. God in His goodness may pull the props out from everything that is holding us together and let us see how much we need Him. He loves us too much to permit life to run so smoothly that we never feel a need for Christ.

One person told me, "There is as much difference in my life since I learned to praise God for everything as there was when I was first filled with the Holy Spirit. Praise has completely changed my attitude. I haven't experienced a moment of unrest since I learned to praise and thank God for everything. Praise has given me more peace of mind than I ever had before."

You will keep him in perfect peace, whose mind is stayed on You, because he trusts in You (Isaiah 26:3 NKJV).

ANSWER TO YOUR PRAISE

This letter isn't an answer to my praise, but it sure is an answer to your praise. For ten years I did everything I could think of to help my husband accept Christ. I prayed, believed, fasted, and prayed some more. I left pieces of literature where I hoped he would read them, but he never did. I attended clinics on how to be a good wife and was as loving to my husband as I knew how to be.

My efforts helped us to get along great, but my husband seemed further from accepting

Christ than ever. Then I heard how a wife had given *Prison to Praise* to her husband. It was the first Christian book he had ever read. I decided to get a copy and try that. To my delight, my husband saw the book and started reading it. I literally held my breath while I prayed he would keep reading. He read the entire book before he got out of his chair! Even after he was through, I didn't say a word for fear I would disrupt whatever God was doing. The next day he said,"What do you think about that book?"

I said, "What book?" "The one about the Army Chaplain. Do you think those things really happened?"

We talked about the book for a long while, and he discovered that he had a new interest in finding out what it was to be a Christian. He soon accepted Christ and was then filled with the Holy Spirit. Thank you for praising the Lord!

My Comments

At the center of every man, there is a desire for praise. God built this desire into his creation. We can misdirect or misuse the desire, but it is still an instinct created by God. When a man hears or reads about praise to God, it touches the instinct within him even when he does not realize what is happening to him. This arouses an interest and often leads to his being released from the outward facade of unconcern.

If you cannot get someone to read a book on praise, you still have a powerful tool you can use. Simply live a life of praise. Being filled with a daily attitude of praise and joy will reach another person's heart even when they do not know what you are doing. If you are irritable, cross and critical, you push people away from God. If you are at peace, joyful and considerate, they will be drawn toward God. But don't expect instant results. People who have seen professing Christians demonstrating the fleshly characteristics of non-Christians, are not likely to respond immediately to your spirit of praise.

Wives, fit in with your husband's plans; for then if they refuse to listen when you talk to them about the Lord, they will be won by your respectful, pure behavior. Your godly lives will speak to them better than any words (1 Peter 3:1-2 TLB).

BORN DAMAGED

Your book *Power in Praise* is right on. I'm a junior in high school, and am really turned on for Christ. When I read your book about praising God for everything that has happened, I could hardly believe it. When I was born, I suffered brain damage that affected my ability to walk. I couldn't see how I could praise God for that. I sure hadn't in the past! I always wondered why God let me be born, if I had to be a cripple. Even after I was a Christian, I wished I hadn't been born.

When I tried doing what you said to do - boy, I couldn't believe what happened to me. I got so excited I could hardly stand it. When I thanked God for my problem, I started feeling like I was the luckiest person in the whole wide world. That was several months ago, and I'm still on cloud nine. I used to have to try and cheer myself up, but now I have to hold my laughter down. I feel so great I can hardly stand it! What has happened to me?

My Comments

This young man was carrying around the heavy burden of complaining against God. When he got rid of that by praising Him, he was relieved of a great hindrance. Now he is free to grow in Christ. As he continues to praise God for everything, He will give him many new joys. The burden of complaining is far greater than most people realize. Satan uses it to dump all kinds of sadness upon us. If there are times when you have a heavy heart, it can probably be traced to your complaining about something. You may feel your complaint is justified, but is it worth the sadness that clings to you? Is God unfair to want you to be filled with the same joy His Son had?

Let all those rejoice who put their trust in You; let them ever shout for joy (Psalm 5:11 NKJV).

REPUTATION ATTACKED

I don't know how it started, but an ugly rumor was destroying my reputation. It was being spread all over my community, and the members of my congregation were hearing it everywhere. It was evident to me that they were thinking, "Where there is smoke, there must be fire." My church board asked me to meet with them and expressed their great concern over the things they were hearing about their pastor. The leaders of my denomination invited me to come and share with them the accusations being made about me.

The rumors were such that there seemed to be no way of pinning them down. No one seemed to know where they originated. For weeks I went through real hell. Daily and sometimes hourly, I gave it over to the Lord and promised I would trust Him to work it out. By the next day I was wrestling with the problem again. It seemed to me that if God was going to let the rumor persist, I should get out of the ministry for good, and yet I knew God had called me to preach. The more I tried to decide what to do, the more confused I became.

Then a dear brother brought me your two books, *Prison to Praise* and *Power in Praise*. He said, "If anyone ever needed these books, you do." Reading books didn't appeal to me at the time, but I agreed to look at them. After a few pages, my attention was so captured that I couldn't put the books down.

By the last page, I knew what had to be done. I couldn't merely accept the problem, I had to praise God for it. This, I confess, was a real battle for me, but God helped me, and I was able to honestly thank Him for everything exactly as it was. At that very moment, God spoke to me more clearly than I had ever heard Him speak before. He said, "You had to be broken that you might be of better service to Me. Now that you understand what it feels like, you are prepared to serve Me in a new way."

From that day on, miracles began to happen in my ministry that I had never seen before. People were healed and filled with the Holy Spirit in astounding ways. I could see people's attitudes toward me changing. They seemed to be saying, "God wouldn't use you as He is if those rumors were true."

Praise the Lord for revealing through you the glorious truth of praise.

My Comments

As painful as it may be, God sometimes will permit Satan to destroy even our reputation. Jesus became "of no reputation" in order that He might suffer unjustly for our sake. We should not be surprised when we are shot at by arrows of accusation. Our human reasoning may insist that an unspotted reputation would be far more effective than one held in question, but God knows what He wants to do with us. There are people He wants to reach who would close their ears to anyone except the man or woman God is making out of you. He loves those people and wants to reach them regardless of what the cost may be. He permitted His own Son to die a shameful death on a cross between two thieves, and He will permit you and me to endure whatever He knows will help others. Our praise and trust open wide the door for Him to use us according to His own plan.

And the God of all grace, who called you to His eternal glory in Christ, after you have suffered a little while, will Himself restore you and make you strong, firm and steadfast (I Peter 5:10 NIV).

MY WIFE LEFT ME

Since I read your books, I have been trying to thank God that my wife left me, but I can't do it. Every time I think about her, I do nothing but cry. I'm getting less and less able to do my work, and I don't even care. I seldom eat a full meal, and I'm never hungry. How can I be thankful that I feel so terrible? I'm not able to help anyone else, and I would like to use my life for something worthwhile.

When my wife first left me, friends told me I would get over it with time. But time is making me worse. I love my wife, and the longer she is gone, the more I miss her. Shouldn't people who love someone be sad when they leave? There are many times that I do wrong, but I don't feel wrong about missing my wife. Do you think I am wrong? You help many people - can you help me?

My Answer

Yes, you are wrong, my friend. You are permitting Satan to destroy you. You believe your sorrow is "right," so you carefully hold on to it. When you realize that it is wrong, you will let go of it and God will give you a new life.

It is wrong to doubt God regardless of the circumstances. It may be natural not to want pain of any kind, just as it is natural not to want separation from someone we love. But even Jesus *learned obedience by the things which he suffered* (Hebrews 5:8). If you want your situation to be used by God to bless you and others, begin to thank Him that your wife is gone. At first it may seem impossible, but do your best and God will honor that. He only requires you to do what you are able to do.

It isn't your wife's departure that is killing you, it is your own reaction to it. God permits you to react however you choose, but He will give you peace if you will thank Him that everything is just as it is and trust Him to work good out of it exactly as He promised. What good? Only He knows the good that needs to be done, and this must be left to Him.

I will be in prayer with you that the Holy Spirit will help you to believe that God is with you and has a perfect plan for your life.

He Wrote Again:
When I received your letter, my reaction was "You're nuts!" I kept on feeling sorry for myself. But your prayer must have gotten through! I went back and read *Power in Praise* again and decided to give praise a good try. At first I felt like a real hypocrite, but once I got started, I knew I had to either make it that time or I would never try it again. I kept on saying, "Thank

You, God." After a while, I could tell that I was feeling a little bit better. When I was convinced that I was a little better, I got excited. God was actually doing something former

You were right. My self-pity gradually left. I saw that I needed God much more than I needed my wife. I still love her and want her, but I'm learning what it means to need God, too. He has a plan for my life, so I am going to enjoy finding out what it is. Several times lately, I've seen an opportunity to do something for someone else, and I actually enjoyed doing it. When I was crying like a baby, I thought only of myself. It is like I was in a fog and am now starting to see the sunshine. Please keep praying for me. God must have more things He wants to do in me.

My Comments

It will take a lifetime for God to complete His plan for our lives. When that plan is completed, we are then ready for heaven. In heaven we will be relieved of all our problems, but here on earth we need to experience whatever suffering will fit us for the eternal plan He has for us. Each of us is being prepared to serve Him in our own special way for all eternity. God could have started our eternity in heaven with the angels, but we were to come here first and learn whatever we needed to know. If we choose to grumble and fight against His will for us, we will be like the man who beats his head against a stone wall. That really isn't the purpose for a wall. Doubting God isn't the purpose for life either!

I know that You can do all things. No plan of Yours can be thwarted (Job 42:2 NIV).

POLIO

I deeply appreciated your letter and I'm sorry I didn't acknowledge it sooner. I have read and re-read it many times. I had always thought I was a good Christian (Catholic), but until I read your books, I did not have the faith I have now. I have prayed to God for over fifty years, but I don't believe that I ever praised Him for my infirmities before (I had polio at the age of two). I know that polio made me a stronger person, as I have had to struggle for many things. God has blessed me in many ways and now I am thanking Him for my infirmity as well as asking Him to heal me.

I have been attending prayer meetings, and have discovered that by praying with others, I have become closer to God. Since your letter, I have the faith and the confidence that some day He will heal my leg. I feel it so strongly. At two of the prayer meetings, I felt His closeness, and for the first time I actually have had tears in my eyes. After my husband's death, leaving me with two young sons to raise, I withheld tears so long that I didn't think it was possible for them to start coming again. My work is more pleasant, too. I can overlook gossip, unpleasantness in the surroundings, and just praise Him.

Thank you for writing to me, and may God give you the strength to continue imparting faith to others.

My Comments

Tears have been "shut off" by some who have permitted grief to overcome them. Others in self-pity cry nearly continually. In either case, the sufferer is shutting off the peace of mind now enjoyed by the writer of this letter. The person guilty of self-pity often feels so completely justified in his sorrow that he highly resents anyone even hinting that his pain is self-imposed.

It is easier to blame suffering on others than it is to accept responsibility and then permit God to do something about it. Problems caused by situations completely beyond our human control do not give us license to give in to the agony of self-pity. If we do so, we permit Satan to heap pain upon us that God does not intend for us to bear. If we resist the temptation from Satan to drown ourselves in self-pity, God will abundantly reward us.

Believe that His Son was telling you the truth when He promised to supply all of your needs. Your faith in Christ opens the door for God to do whatever He desires to do in you. The writer of this letter is being transformed by her trust in God. Instead of keeping her eyes on the physical problem, she has realized the good that God is working in her. Her spirit is being healed by God, and her joy is beginning to rise. She is being prepared for eternal life! Satan thought affliction would beat her down, but she has permitted her faith in God's goodness to actually cause the polio to work for her good. I praise the Lord for helping her to see the tremendous power there is in praise.

Submit yourselves therefore to God. Resist the devil and he will flee from you (James 4:7 RSV).

A SHORT JOURNEY

I know there are many women who feel lonely even though they are married. But believe me, the divorced woman is the most desolate.

I'm aware that a widow is very lonely, yet her

husband is "gone." When a woman is divorced, her husband is around, somewhere. He's alive and breathing,but not with his family. It doesn't matter, at this point, who filed for the divorce. The loneliness is devastating. But praise the Lord, it doesn't have to be devastating. I know. Precious Jesus. I am divorced. I've felt so alone, almost to the point of a mental breakdown. Now, I've found what I was looking for. I've found joy, peace - without resentment. Praise God! I've found out what real Christianity is.

What is it like, being divorced? A few months ago I would have said it's the most terrible, horrible feeling in the world. I'm not condoning divorce, but it does happen. And there you are with nothing - or so you think! It does not have to be that way. Praise the Lord! If anyone feels alone for any reason, please tell them about me. Especially if they are divorced. Beg them to listen. I have been divorced three years. In that time, I've reached the absolute bottom of despair. I've seen my ex-husband marry the woman who helped destroy our marriage, and my children have been given to them by the court because they could offer "a more stable home atmosphere with two parents in the home."

I was living in California during this part of my life. I called my mother in Florida one day and told her I thought I was cracking up. I was walking a tightrope, and I was about to fall off. She told me to pray. Well, I tried to pray. Nothing happened. Then one day, a large envelope came in the mail from Mom. Inside was a copy of *Prison to Praise* by Merlin Carothers. I read it and then re-read it. I called Mom.

"I'm just not too sure," I told her, "what I think about that book."

Then my mother sent me your book, *Power in Praise*. Praise God. That finally got me started. I praised God for everything I could think of - my divorce, the children being with their daddy, everything. My whole attitude changed. A friend of mine said to me, "What's happened with you? There's such a glow on your face." And that was before I received the Holy Spirit. Praise the Lord.

I went home to work for my father and began the most wonderful journey of my life - to the Holy Spirit and Jesus. One week after I arrived, I received the Baptism of the Holy Spirit. I had been a chain smoker for two years, smoking two packs a day. The night I received the Baptism, I had the nicotine habit taken from me. I've not wanted a cigarette since! Thank You, Jesus.

I've put the lives of my children in the Lord's hands. He has heard me. I don't know how He is doing it, I don't question it, I just know He is sending my children to me. In the meantime, I praise Him for letting them be with their daddy and his wife.

I feel at peace. I feel joy. I've seen miracles. My own dad, for one. He's been healed of two gastric ulcers and a hiatal hernia. Praise God. There is no need for anyone to worry or feel alone. None whatsoever! They can trust Him, step out in faith. Every sorrow and care will be gone. Hallelujah. The journey from darkness into light is so short. Once it's been made, the life left behind seems so long ago.

My Comments

A flick of a switch, and light floods a dark room. A sudden realization that God will use each detail of every experience in our life to bless us, and an inner light comes on. The despair of inward darkness is gone, and the peace of God moves in.

Thank You, God, for providing this unfailing answer to every problem. Please help us to share it with as many people as possible.

Never will I leave you; Never will I forsake you (Hebrews 13:5 NIV).

I ASKED FOR THE BAPTISM

I have prayed for the Baptism in the Holy Spirit and have been aching to receive it. I am surprised to hear other people say they do not want to speak in tongues, for I would be glad to do this or anything God wanted me to do. Others have prayed for me several times, but I have received nothing. My question is, "How can I possibly praise the Lord that I have not received what I know would help me to be a better witness for Christ?"

My Comments

Many people are confused about what the Baptism in the Holy Spirit is and are guilty of disbelieving Christ's promises. In Luke 11:13 Jesus promised: *If you then...know how to give good gifts to your children, how much more shall your heavenly Father give the Holy Spirit to those who ask Him?* This is a simple straightforward promise that many people have tried to complicate. Jesus meant it when He said, *Ask with your heart, and God will provide.*

"But I haven't spoken in tongues yet," many have told me. "Isn't speaking in tongues one of the signs I should receive?" Yes, this is correct if the emphasis is placed on the word "should." Our lack of faith can hold back this gift, but that does not nullify Christ's promise. When you have earnestly asked God to baptize you in the Holy Spirit, believe that He has. Believe that all the gifts of the Spirit are dwelling within you and will be made manifest according to your faith. If someone asks, "Have you received the Baptism?" your answer should be, "Yes, I have!" This is a step of faith that God will surely honor. Thank Him for what He has done, and then praise Him. Let your praise be in your heart and on your lips.

If someone asks you, "Have you received a new language?" your answer should be a strong positive "Yes." This is merely confirming what Jesus said: *And these signs shall follow them that believe;...they shall speak with new tongues* (Mark 16:17). We are not supposed to require evidence before we believe His promises. Rejoice in your heart, and know that God has given you through His Spirit the new language He wants you to have, plus the freedom to use all the gifts of the Spirit as the need arises.

What should you say if someone asks you at this point, "Have you ever prayed in tongues?" You should give a firm unembarrassed, "No, I haven't used my new prayer language yet, but I believe God has given it to me."

God always honors this kind of faith. Keep your heart and mind open to listen to His Spirit within you. You will soon hear words that do not, at first, mean anything to you. Open your mouth and speak them. You may explode in joy, or you may feel nothing. You are being obedient to Christ, and He will take care of the feelings in His own time. He wants you first to grow in faith. The Baptism in the Holy Spirit was designed by God to help you grow in your walk with the Lord. Satan may whisper to you, "You only made those words up in your mind." Quickly give your mind to God and tell Him,"Father, You have my mind, and I want You to use it for Your glory."

Then proceed to let the Holy Spirit use your tongue to talk to God. You may have one word, or many. The numbers are unimportant. Your faith in Christ is what is important. It was through faith in Christ that you received eternal life. It is through faith in Christ that God gives you His Baptism in the Holy Spirit.

When Abraham believed Him, God promised to use him to build a mighty nation. God's plan has always been for man to believe Him. Whenever He finds a man or woman who will believe, He pours out His blessings upon them. Speaking in tongues is a result of your faith in God. You believe, and God gives. He does not give sparingly or grudgingly, but He can give only to those who will believe and trust Him.

If you have been honestly seeking the

Baptism in the Holy Spirit, and you know that Christ is your Savior, you can at this moment believe that His promise is fulfilled in you. Do not doubt for any reason, and soon "rivers of living water" will be flowing from within you.

Jesus stood and cried out, saying "If anyone thirsts, let him come to Me, and drink. He who believes in me, as the Scripture has said, Out of his heart will flow rivers of living water" (John 7:37-38 NKJV).

Faith is the substance of things hoped for, the evidence of things not seen (Hebrews 11:1 KJV).

HE CAN DO IT FOR ANYBODY

In 1970, sometime toward the end of the year, my pastor played your tape from a FGBM meeting. Later a friend had the tape, and I listened to it again, but since my problems at the time were so enormous, I had little understanding.

A few weeks after my husband left me with a three-year-old and seven-week-old baby, I was told of your book. A friend offered to take me to the bookstore that day, and I bought the last copy of *Prison to Praise.* I read it through in a few hours. For the next three days, even with tears and an aching heart, I praised God.

Nothing happened until the night of the third day. While I was thinking about God, something inside me broke, and I began to bubble, then laugh and laugh. This lasted for three days, and when I "came down," it was to normal, not the horrible depression I had before.

Then, through the horrible nightmarish days that followed, I tried to keep praising God and giving thanks in obedience to His Word. I had put so many barriers up that God had to pull them down to get through to me. Having been absolutely broken, I nearly lost my mind, but God was holding on to it. Then I set my mind to feed on His Word. As often as I had coffee, I read His Word, mainly the Psalms. I saw that no matter how David felt, or what was going on, he ended up praising God. As I praised, I was filled with joy - His joy. The joy healed my mind. I was 100 percent better after the first week.

About six weeks later, I bought *Power in Praise*, and was thrilled that you were teaching about some of the things God had taught me. God gave me understanding as to what He had done in my life - and why. I thought my world had come to an end when my husband turned his back on God; now I have hope and the faith and trust to let God work. Nothing can happen to the three of us without God's allowing it. And whatever happens will bring glory to Him, and blessing to us.

I don't know if you can appreciate to the fullest what God has done, because it's hard to tell how bad life was for me. I gave up many times and twice tried suicide. Certainly it was the Holy Spirit that protected and sustained me. Because I've survived through so many problems, I can understand others, and tell them that I know praising God works. I've done it - rather, God's done it in me for His glory.

Many times I have had to make myself swallow tears and say, "Praise the Lord!" Just last Friday I arrived at work and found I no longer had a job. I said, "Praise the Lord!" It was my first thought and response. That's what God has done for me. I know if God can make a happy Christian out of me, He can do it for anybody.

My Comments

No sudden change in the situation, nothing radical. Just a growing assurance that God is watching over us. This is the best result we can have in praising God! Most people are excited about the abrupt transforming power of praise. It excites me, too, but I'm even more excited over the possibility of growing in solid faith in God. This faith demands no outward manifestation of

God's power. It says, "God I trust You whether You change my situation or not." Rejoice if you have learned that God trusts you to trust Him!

Those who sow in tears shall reap in joyful shouting (Psalm 126:5 NASB).

EYES OFF PROBLEM

We find ourselves in dire financial difficulty. It is hard for us, faced with more bills than we can pay, to keep our eyes off our problems and upon Christ.

I have promised the Lord that I will praise Him in all things if He will teach me how. I do realize already that He has permitted our difficulty to bring us into a closer walk with Him.

Since we have brought many of our problems upon ourselves, it is a relief to know that God is in charge and that He has permitted all of them for our good and His Glory. It removes the burden of guilt, which kept coming back even though we had confessed our sins and knew we were forgiven.

Please pray for us that we will remain constant in praise and thanksgiving, no matter what. We do accept the fact that it is the will of God for us to give thanks in everything. Once you see it, there's no getting around it!

My Comments

The temptation to keep our eyes on the problem rather than on praising God is often overpowering. As a result, we amplify the problem rather than finding the solution.

Many people today are in financial difficulty. (Some for reasons beyond their control). Others, like these folks, because they have not been wise stewards of their money. Books by Larry Burkett and Ron Blue are excellent resources to learn how to wisely handle our finances. They can be found in Christian bookstores.

What does God have to say about the prosperity of His people? Does He even care? If we want to be prosperous, Deuteronomy 29:9 and Joshua 1:7 instruct us to be careful to obey His Word. Psalm 1 tells us that the man who delights in and meditates on God's Word will prosper.

The Lord be magnified, who has pleasure in the prosperity of His servant (Psalm 35:27 NKJV).

FOUNDATION OF PRAISE

In your book you write about giving your books to men in prison. I would like to have a part in work like that. Please let me know how much you need at this time, and I will do my best to help.

My Answer

The need for books to give those in prison is unlimited. Few people realize how many men as well as women and young people are behind bars.

To supply books for hospitals and servicemen would require millions of dollars. However, we are not responsible for what we cannot do. God only asks us to do what we can. I do know that for the price of one book, many prisoners have accepted Christ as Savior and are now doing their best to lead others to Christ.

God will take our best and multiply it many times over. Please ask Him what you should do.

The Lord loves a cheerful giver (II Corinthians 9:7 NIV).

AN ARMY GENERAL

Nearly all of my adult life has been spent in trying to make the Army the professional and effective force I believe it should be. I advanced in rank, for God gave me a good mind and the ability to concentrate on details.

I woke up one day to realize that my

dedication to the Army had cost me far more than I realized. My wife no longer cared anything for me. My two sons resented everything I said or did. I responded with bitterness and self-pity, and things got even worse. My wife's poodle was the only member of the family who seemed to care anything about me.

Our post chaplain brought me your book *Prison to Praise*, and urged me to read it. I promised him I would, just to get him off my back. I didn't know what I was getting into! Your life and ideas hit me in the pit of my stomach. I realized that there was something to religion that I had never known anything about. I never would have tried your ideas on praising God if it hadn't been for the fantastic stories you told. I decided you either had to be a big liar or the discoverer of something I needed.

I started thanking God for my life and home as it was. To my amazement, one of my sons came in that night and said, "Hi, Dad. How are things?" That might sound very trivial to some people, but to me it was a sign. I kept thanking God. Things kept happening right and left - things I could hardly believe.

I know you must receive thousands of letters, but I wanted to tell you that as a result of praising God, my entire life has changed. I have a family now. We enjoy life together. I'm seeking God's will in many ways.

I'm very proud to share your books with others, and I've urged the post chaplain to get as many as he can.

My Comments

Men at every level of our society are being drawn to God. It may come as a surprise to some of you former military personnel that God loves generals, too!

A lifetime of mistaken priorities can mean the death of what should be a happy family. No amount of self-incrimination can change what has already been done. But God has the sovereign power to overcome the most awful mistakes when we praise Him. Men who have solved the most complex problems in their profession are often stymied in their efforts to get out of the prison of unhappiness in their homes. God alone holds the answer to this problem, and He has revealed it to us through the principle of thanking and praising God for everything that happens to us. Strange as it may seem, praise and thanksgiving to the Lord hold the key to victorious Christian living.

In all these things we are more than conquerors through Him who loved us (Romans 8:37 RSV).

———————

IN PRISON

I have just finished reading *Prison to Praise*, here in prison. I felt the power of God as I read what He did in your life.

I thank God for guiding you to write such a Spirit-filled book. It has changed me so that I am able to accept my own life. I never thought I could be glad to be where I am, but now I can honestly say, "Praise You, Lord, for getting me into prison!" I know it was the Lord's will to bring me here. I know He has a work for me to do, and I am thankful that He arranged whatever was necessary to get me started.

I wonder how I would have been, had I met you when I was in the Army. When I was in Vietnam, I became addicted to drugs. I was given an undesirable discharge. From there, I went into armed robbery to support my habit. Praise God, I got arrested and sentenced to a four-year term in prison. After my arrival here, another prisoner led me to accept Christ. I have found a real happiness and joy in Jesus as Lord. Never again will I be lonely or feel unloved.

I praise God for the blessings He has bestowed upon all His children. Please include me in your prayers, and always thank God that I am here, for here I received eternal life. Whenever Satan decides to give me a rough time, I remind him that it was within these stone walls that I was delivered from his prison. The guards cannot understand why I am so filled with joy. Frequently I see them looking at me as if they wonder what has happened to me. Whenever I get the opportunity, I tell them that Jesus has happened to me.

My Comments

Do you believe that God can change whatever "prison" Satan has built around you, into a place of joy? The more difficult your situation happens to be, the more powerful will be the change that God will work in you through His Son, Jesus. Any self-pity that you may feel, for whatever reason, is a testimony that you do not believe that Jesus came into this world to set you free from all bondage. The Psalmist cried: *Bring my soul out of prison that I may praise Your Name* (Psalm 142:7). And that's exactly what Jesus has done for us. Speaking prophetically, Isaiah tells us that God has anointed Him (Christ) to bind up and heal the broken hearted, to proclaim freedom for both the physical and spiritual captives, and release from darkness for those held prisoners by the enemy (see Isaiah 61:1 AMP).

MY APPETITE

My husband is a compulsive drinker. He drinks to feel good, to forget his problems. I keep telling him that God will solve our problems if he will quit drinking, but I can't get through to him. I hate drinking and I know it isn't God's will. Please pray that he will quit.

I want to honor God in every way possible. But one thing I have not been able to overcome is my appetite. I am unable to control it. I gain more and more weight and I know this does not please God, but what can I do?

My Comments

Millions of people are asking God to control appetites of one kind or another that have become their prisons. If you have this problem, let me share a very powerful secret with you. Your appetite may indeed be so strong that you cannot make it go away. But there is one thing you do have the power to do! Stop gratifying the appetite!

"But I feel so bad if I don't gratify my appetite," you say. Go ahead and feel bad. God will not heal your appetite while you are doing everything you can to make it worse. But He will heal the appetite if you will let go of it long enough for Him to make it well.

This woman sees her own appetite for food as uncontrollable, but her husband's appetite for drink as controllable. Both problems come from the individual's unwillingness to do what God has given us the power to do. When we do our part, He will take care of the part we can do nothing about.

The glorious thing is that God loves us whether we do our part or not. If we want to grow fat and die from obesity, He will forgive us. Thank God, He provides the answers to our needs but doesn't condemn us if we are too weak to accept His answers.

Do you have an appetite for something you know is hurting you? You can - right now through Christ - stop satisfying it long enough for God to heal you. How long does it take? As long as it takes for you to believe He has done it!

For the kingdom of God is not meat and drink; but righteousness, and peace, and joy in the Holy Ghost (Romans 14:17 KJV).

A POINT OF CONTACT

What a bombshell your books have been to us! It seems like everything is embodied in praise. The Holy Spirit is surely using it to speak to us. The way many people are centering their attention on praise, indicates that these must be the last days.

I worship in a fundamental Bible church where they do not talk much about praising the Lord. I plan to put your books in the church library. Praise and thank the Lord with me for what He will do.

I discovered several testimonies that fit me in *Answers to Praise*. I decided that instead of just "reading and enjoying" the book that I should make each letter, and your teaching, as a point of contact with God's promises.

As I did, I found nearly every article had something of value for my life.

My Comments

A few people have written saying, "I have read your first three books and enjoyed them." They then go to explain in detail their own problems, as if they had not comprehended what they read in my first three books.

How refreshing it is to see that this reader has listened to what God has taught others and has used their experiences to strengthen her own life. We might just as well profit from the mistakes of others. We aren't going to live long enough to make them all ourselves!

These things happened to them as examples and were written down as warnings for us (I Corinthians 10:11 NIV).

SUICIDE

I went to a hotel and rented a room with one purpose in mind. I wanted a private place to take my life. When the bell boy left, I started my preparations. I sat at a desk to write my farewell letter to the world I hated so much.

On the desk was a bright colored book that caught my eyes, *Prison to Praise*. I had been in prison, so I picked it up to see what another poor soul might have been through.

As I read your story, my eyes filled with tears, and I couldn't put it down.

Your story did something to me that I thought would never happen. It made me believe there was a God!

Lying on the floor and asking God to do something for me, I heard a voice that said, "Look for a Bible." I got up and found one there in the room. On the first page I opened to, I saw "You must be born again." I didn't know what it meant, but I asked God to do that for me, and something happened inside. I began to laugh like I never had laughed before in all my life.

Suddenly I was so happy I wanted to tell the whole world what God had done for me. I went down to the lobby and tried to tell someone. Everyone acted as if they thought I was drunk. I went back to my room and read the Bible all night. I didn't know it was such a great Book!

Thank you for writing your book. It saved my life. Or, it gave me a new one. Now I can even praise God for the old one.

My Comments

Many of us know that the Bible is God's Holy Word. But it isn't much use to tell this to many others. If they don't believe us, they will not read it. If they do believe, they might say "So what?" and still never read it.

We need to get books into people's hands that will help them to believe that the Bible has the answer to their needs! I may never know who placed that copy of *Prison to Praise* in a hotel room, but whoever you are, "Thank you." Do you know of a hotel, motel, prison, hospital, or military post where there are people who need to be "turned on" to the Bible and set free from their prison?

Jesus came to give to us: *the oil of gladness instead of mourning, and a garment of praise instead of a spirit of despair* (Isaiah 61:3 NIV).

A PRISON GUARD

I've asked myself a thousand times why I ever decided to become a prison guard. I believe it is the hardest job a man could have. For eleven years I wondered each day I came to work if that would be the day I would get a knife in my back.

I think everyone likes to work in a pleasant place, but this place has been anything but pleasant. We've been overcrowded and poorly equipped ever since I have been here. The prisoners have always been angry and seemed on the edge of riot. We've had to be on constant alert, and I usually went home dead tired. I took my weariness and frustrations and fears out on my family, and even being at home was like being in another prison.

Then I noticed that one of the prisoners had a complete change of attitude. He was getting his food one day when I saw him smile and say, "Praise the Lord." The food was especially bad that day, and I wondered what he was planning. I watched him carefully to see what he might do next. As he ate, he kept on smiling as if he knew something good was going to happen. Naturally this worried me, so I told the other guards to be on their toes.

This went on for several days, and then I heard another man saying, "Praise the Lord," when he was assigned a job none of the men liked. My curiosity got the better of me, and I asked him, "Why did you say that?"

He said, "I read a book that Joe has, and I'm feeling better already."

Joe was the man I had noticed first. I went to him and asked to see the book. It was *Prison to Praise*. I looked to see if it was approved by the librarian. He had signed it.

When my curiosity couldn't stand it any longer, I asked Joe to let me read his book. It had been read so often that adhesive tape held the pages together, but I got the message.

From that time on, I've noticed a continuing change in this entire block. More and more men come to work singing. They laugh and joke. I come to work feeling good, and go home feeling even better.

If you can spare more copies of *Prison to Praise* I will be glad to share them with other parts of this prison. The chaplain says he isn't supposed to solicit anything for free, but no one has told me I can't do it.

God bless you. If you are helping others like you have helped me and the men here, please keep it up. I've been going to church all my life, but I've never believed in God like I do now.

My Comments

There are very few correctional institutions in our country that have happy people in them. Overcrowding, insufficient staff, and unhealthy living conditions are common. But the heart of the problem is men and women without hope of ever finding anything better. Nearly every man was unhappy when he went in, and in spite of his most optimistic dreams, he knows that life will be even tougher when he gets out. What incentive does he have to do better? Usually none. "Religion" may be a dirty word to him, but he will respond to the love of Jesus. Anything we can do to reach into his heart with the good news of the Gospel will be rewarded.

Recently I sent a large supply of *Prison to Praise* to this guard. He has since told me that there is a spiritual move in his prison more powerful than anything he has seen on the outside.

Repent then, and turn to God, so that your sins may be wiped out, that times of refreshing may come from the Lord (Acts 3:19 NIV).

———————

I BEGAN TO SEARCH

Six months ago, as our marriage began to go on the rocks, I started searching for God's will. My husband, our seven-year-old daughter, and I were at a major crossroad.

There was another woman in my husband's life. I was floored. I had never expected such a thing to happen. I thought we were so devoted to each other. Our friends were also flabbergasted. Our marriage seemed the most perfect in our crowd.

I did my best to get my husband to stay with me, but he refused, claiming that he loved the other woman. When he moved in with her, I tried to trust the Lord. It wasn't easy.

They had lived together for a week when, *Power in Praise*, was given to me. After a few pages I praised the Lord for all of this in my life. I thanked Him for the other woman. I thanked Him that my husband had left me. The Holy Spirit blessed and overwhelmed me, and I felt as if I were speaking in a new language.

I kept on searching for God's will. I filed for divorce, and the papers were served on my husband Tuesday night of this week. I never expected to see him again, as I knew his anger toward me would be terrible. But the next day he came to see me. We really talked, and he told me many things I had been doing for years that irked him. I saw God telling me many things.

Now my husband wants to come home! Praise the God who loves us!

I have lots of doubts and fears, in a way. But I know that God can and will work everything out for our good. The battle is God's, not mine, and He knows best. I know that He is going to show us great and mighty things. I stand expectantly upon the promise He gave me in Jeremiah 33:3: *Call unto me, and I will...show thee great and mighty things.* I do praise God for everything.

My Comments

What will the outcome be? The important thing is that another child of God has made a step toward trusting Him rather than the conditions of their life. Think of the power there is in praising God - the blessing of His presence, His joy and peace. Is it any wonder that God permits events that will help us learn to praise Him? There is nothing like adversity to force us to learn what it means to trust God! He knows this, whether you and I understand or not. He will allow Satan to stir up whatever trouble will cause us to recognize our need to walk closer to Him. When adversity is raging, the human being often thinks, "If God would solve this problem,

I would really be happy." But this isn't true. We find our joy in praising and rejoicing in Him.

Come to Me, all you who labor and are heavy laden, and I will give you rest. Take My yoke upon you and learn from Me, for I am gentle and lowly in heart, and you will find rest for your souls. For My yoke is easy and My burden is light (Matthew 11:29 NKJV).

HAPPY IN PRISON

The chaplain here at Los Angeles County Jail gave me *Prison to Praise* and *Power in Praise.* When I finished reading them I invited Jesus into my heart as "my personal Savior." Anyhow I heard those words somewhere, and they sound like what happened to me. Jesus is personal to me now. I know He saves me from my sins.

On the same day, I had here in my cell what you call the Baptism in the Holy Spirit. It was as if my mind became alive again. I'm free in Christ. God has set me free in jail! On the outside, I was always in prison. I'm only twenty-one but it seems as if I have been in prison for a hundred years. I was always mad at someone for making life so miserable for me. Now I know it wasn't people who made me miserable. It was the devil, and I didn't even believe in Him!

Unless God changes things, I'll be behind bars for a long while, but don't feel sorry for me. I'm the happiest I've been in all my life. For the first time I'm glad to be alive. The policeman who busted me would never believe what a favor he did for me!

There are many unhappy people here, and I'm trying to help them. I'll be moving to a new place soon, and I know God will make it the right place. Pray that my coming days will help others to be thankful and to know our Savior.

My Comments

When I begin a new day, I often think of the men behind bars who are praying for an opportunity to tell someone about Jesus. Their freedom is limited, and they must be ready to give a few words of the "Good News" when the opportunity comes. When that moment passes, the fellow prisoner will move onto his own private prison. If you have unlimited opportunities to move about and share Christ with others, please pray that God will give you a heart to respond to every opportunity.

Preach the word! Be ready in season and out of season...for the time will come when they will not endure sound doctrine (II Timothy 4:2-3 NKJV).

———————

CRYING IN PRISON

I hope you get this letter. I read *Prison to Praise* here in jail. I will be going to prison after my trial, for I'm guilty and will admit it. I know I have to pay for what I did, but I know the Lord will help me do it the best way possible.

I feel strange after writing that last sentence. I've never written or spoken about the Lord before, and I can hardly believe it's me writing!

Christians were a big nothing to me before I came here. Their big churches and fancy clothes turned me off. I didn't have anything decent, and couldn't understand why I was always so poor. I was mad about many other things, too.

Then the man in the cell next to me handed me a book a few days ago and said, "You need this more than I did." When I saw it was something about religion, I didn't want to read it, but I didn't have anything else to read. The more I read it, the crazier I felt. I can't remember when I ever cried before that, but I sure made up for lost time. I wasn't unhappy, either.

You had been like me. You had found a way out. I started knowing that I could, too. What a feeling that was! I had hope for the first time that life could be better for me.

While I was reading *Prison to Praise*, the fellow who gave it to me hollered, "What do you think of it?" I couldn't answer him right away, because I didn't want him to know I had been crying. But when I didn't answer, he guessed why. "Are you crying, too?" he asked me.

I was able to get out, "What do you mean?" He said, "I know; I cried the whole way through it."

After I finished the book, we talked about our past lives, and then he said, "Could we do it too?"

"Do what?"

"Become churchgoers."

"No," I said, "that isn't for me. I don't want to be a churchgoer." Then he said he didn't want to either, but he wanted to be different from what he had been. We talked until we agreed that what we wanted was to become Christians. I don't know if we did anything right or not, but something really happened to us. I *know* I'm a Christian now. I'm *glad* I came to jail! I'm glad for all the things that happened to you, sir, and glad for everything that brought me here.

If you have more books, please send them to me. I'll share them with the fellow in the next cell. He still has many problems, but we keep saying, "Praise the Lord," and he hasn't complained once since we believed in God and Jesus.

My Comments

Yes, more books are on the way. People all over the United States are providing them for this man, and others like him. I'm pleased that he didn't decide to become just a "churchgoer." He has found Jesus, and that is far more important. Wherever he goes in prison, there will be many unhappy men whom he can help. He belongs to God now, and the Holy Spirit will give him the right words to minister the transforming power of the good news about Jesus.

Do not be anxious beforehand what you are to say; but say whatever is given you in that hour, for it is not you who speak, but the Holy Spirit (Mark 13:11 RSV).

PLEASE STAY HUMBLE

As a teacher of young married ladies, I am always seeking ways of growing in "grace and knowledge" that I might help them do the same. (I'm a firm believer that you cannot teach what you do not know, and cannot lead where you will not go.) Therefore, I look for books and helps of all kinds. I have Christian friends with whom I exchange these books. This is how I came to read *Prison to Praise* and *Power in Praise*. How they have changed my life!

The first time reading left me a bit doubtful, the second reading more interested. But by the third time around, I'm convinced. I am now giving your books to others. I have never written to any author before, but felt the Lord wanted me to tell you what a blessing your books have been to me and others. After reading *Answers to Praise*, I felt a real need to pray for you, that you would stay humble and give all the glory to God. May be the thought was unmerited. How easy it would be for you to get puffed up with vain glory from people thanking you and praising you for all your wonderful help. May you continue to be used of the Lord as His servant as long as you live.

My Comments

I am very thankful for those who pray that God will keep me humble. I tremble at the thought of my even starting to think that I am anything important. I know that I am the least deserving of all God's children.

But I am not always praised. Another woman wrote, "I can tell by the way you write that you are extremely proud of yourself."

"Thank You, Lord!"

God chose what is foolish in the world to shame the wise...what is weak...to shame the strong, God chose what is low and despised in the world, even things that are not, to bring to nothing things that are, so that no one might boast in the presence of God (I Corinthians 1:27-29 RSV).

SEARCHING

I am the wife of an alcoholic, a retired Army man. I accepted Christ as a teenager but drifted away through the years. My husband was not a Christian, and it was very easy for me to join the crowd with him. After his retirement, the drinking became worse, and I knew I must get back to God to keep my sanity. My father was a Methodist minister, and I knew that God was my source of strength, but it has not been easy.

For over two years, I struggled to regain the feeling of forgiveness that I knew when I accepted Christ as a teenager. I went to church faithfully, went to the altar often, and prayed and was prayed for by my minister. I joined a special sharing group, and received much peace. But every time my husband went on a drinking bout, I became depressed, filled with anger, panic, hate, and fear. I would lose my feeling of closeness to God.

One morning a couple of weeks ago, I told my minister how I felt, and he handed me your book *Prison to Praise.* He told me not to read it too fast, but I could not put it down. I finished it before I went to sleep that night. Somewhere in the middle of the book, I got out of bed and fell to my knees. I poured out my soul to God and praised Him for my life as it is. I realized that what He had let happen in my life had brought me back to Him. An indescribable peace and joy came over me that I have never known before. The next day was Sunday, and I was so full of joy and love at church. I am praising God for my husband, for his affliction, and asking God to open his eyes to the Truth.

My Comment

"Thank you, pastor, for sharing *Prison to Praise* with this woman. Thank You, God, for helping this wife to believe." If you want God to do things for you, please do not hinge your faith on what He does for you. I know of no quicker way to stop God from working in your life than for you to insist you will believe after He does what you want.

The just shall live by faith (Habakkuk 2:4 KJV).

———————

MY MINISTER

I gave *Prison to Praise* to our minister. When I asked him if he had read it, he said, "Yes, it was a good book. But do you believe in praying in tongues?"

"Yes, I do."

"Please do not distribute that book around the church," he said quite sternly.

"Why?" I asked.

"I believe speaking in tongues is of the devil and I do not want our people reading anything that will make them interested in it."

I was quite taken back, and at first was real angry. Did he think I was going to contaminate the church? Then I realized that by getting angry I was playing into the Devil's hands. I thanked the Lord that my minister was exactly as he was. I believed God would do whatever needed to be done to help him be filled with the Holy Spirit.

I asked several others in our church with whom I had shared your book to meet with me. We agreed to keep praising the Lord for our minister, to help him in every way we could, and to believe God would do something great.

Then an amazing thing happened. The richest and best-loved man of our church received a copy of *Prison to Praise* from his son. He went to the pastor to ask him to read it. When the pastor expressed strong misgivings about the book, he said, "Let's get his other books and see what we think of them." The pastor agreed, and they both read your *Power in Praise* and *Answers to Praise*. The man then contacted me and asked me what I thought of them.

Praise the Lord, I told him how much I loved praising the Lord and how richly God had blessed me since I received the Baptism in the Holy Spirit. I invited him to attend some of our weekly meetings to see what the Lord was doing. Again he went to the pastor and said, "I want to see what is going on within our church. Please go to one of these meetings with me so we can see for ourselves." To our delight, the pastor agreed to come!

You probably know what happened! He came once and then he came back again! He said later he only wanted to come to learn what we were doing wrong! But before long, he asked us to pray for him, and he was baptized in the Holy Spirit! I had never seen him really laugh, but he laughed so long when he received the Baptism that I thought he would never stop.

My Comments

There is a story about a man who stood on the bank of a stream laughing at the people who were in swimming. He got so close, he slipped and fell in!

Thank the Lord for laymen who have learned not to get upset with their minister, and are wise enough to refrain from trying to convince him. They have learned to praise God for their pastor exactly as he is, and to encourage him at every opportunity. Of course, your praise to God may push him into the stream, but isn't that what you want?

Encourage one another and build each other up (I Thessalonians 5:11 NKJV).

I WAS AN ALCOHOLIC

My life was one continuous tangle of drunkenness. I had been in all the jails and hospitals for alcoholics in the Atlanta area. I had a suicidal complex, and my psychiatrist predicted I would jump out of a hotel window. He told my family to write me off as a lost cause. He refused to see me again, since I was drunk every time I went to his office.

Then on a cold sleety Sunday afternoon in March, 1948, a dear saint with a compassionate heart began witnessing to me about Jesus. My teeth chattered with the cold. I was about to shrug him off when he took off his coat, put it around my shoulders, and continued to claim me for Jesus. That impressed me, and I started to pay attention to what he was saying.

Praise God, He who would not let me go. I had already had my throat cut, been stabbed. I strongly believe this was my last chance for salvation. On that day, God gave me complete victory over alcohol, and my life has been wonderful for many years.

Last October I read *Prison to Praise*. (I've bought many copies since then.) Then followed a deep hunger for the Baptism in the Holy Spirit. I read and studied and prayed night and day. When nothing seemed to happen, I carried my Bible to my cabin in the mountains of north Georgia and determined to receive the Baptism or die. I had taught an adult Sunday School class for years, but I was totally ignorant of the part faith plays in the reception of the Holy Spirit. In my cabin on Blood Mountain, God revealed the Truth to me. By faith, I received the Baptism in the Holy Spirit and entered a new dimension of walking in Christ.

My Comment

Since God inhabits the praises of His people, it is very natural for praise to bring a hungering for more of His Spirit. Redeemed alcoholics and people with every kind of infirmity are drawn to His Spirit as they praise God. Those who have been grumbling and complaining are transformed as they learn to fill their mouths with praise and thanksgiving to God.

If you ask anything in My Name, I will do it (John 14:14 NKJV).

OVERWEIGHT

I have one problem that I can't get victory over. I have been overweight since I have been saved. I always thought I could lose weight anytime I wanted to. I was mistaken. I went to doctors, took diet pills, joined clubs, all kinds of diets, and spent lots of money to solve my problem - only to gain more. My conscience bothers me when I eat things I know I shouldn't eat. I try to diet and I cannot.

I really need a miracle from God for the answer. I have thought maybe I'm supposed to be fat, but I do not feel well at all. I'm short of breath, and do not have enough energy to get my work done. It is not good for my heart, among other things, so I'm sure the Lord does not intend for it to be this way. My husband does not like it either.

I'm asking you to pray for me, and believe

with me that the Lord will teach, show, lead, guide, or direct me in this matter. I'm not at all happy about my weight. I think about it all the time, and worry about it continually.

My Answer

Be sure of one thing - God loves you exactly as you are. This is very important for you to understand. You ask for my help. Are you ready to receive advice? It may be hard to receive. Very often I receive letters from wives that read like this, "My husband has always been a strong moral man and a perfect father. He is the last man in the world that I would expect to be unfaithful. But I have just learned that he is having an affair with another woman, and wants a divorce."

In many of these cases, the wife reports that the only problem they had was her weight. She believed she was incapable of controlling her desire for food, yet believed her husband should control his desire to have an attractive appealing wife.

We have the freedom to decide what we want most. We can choose to satisfy our desire to overeat, or we can choose to satisfy our desire to have a happy home and family.

A decision of this kind will be extremely

difficult to make. You need the help that Jesus wants to give you. He died to carry all your "grief." Ask Him to heal you of your excess appetite and believe that He has done it. If you experience symptoms that you are not completely healed, praise God. Rejoice that you are exactly as you are. I believe He is using even your appetite to draw you to Himself.

One woman who was having a struggle with overeating wrote, "I didn't see how praising God could help me stop eating, but I followed your advice and kept praising Him, no matter how I felt. In the midst of an especially difficult time, I received joy that caused me to laugh and laugh. When this was over, I knew God had met a great need within me. I was well! The excessive need to eat left!"

Yes, God is able to do a miracle, and take away our harmful appetites. But He does not always do this. Usually we must choose what we most want to enjoy. Gratifying unhealthy desires, for whatever reason, nearly always results in our losing something that we really want much more. The freedom of choice that God gives us requires us to use wisdom when we select the pleasures we want. His love for us never changes, but when we make the wrong choice, we may have to endure unnecessary suffering.

Now I will break their yoke from your neck and tear your shackles away (Nahum 1:13 NIV).

————————

GOD USES BOOKS

I sent your books to my daughter-in-law. She started reading *Power in Praise*, got up the next Sunday, and went to church. She hadn't gone for almost a year. God filled her with the Holy Spirit, and she is teaching Sunday School now. She is believing God to save her husband and children.

My Comments

Praise the Lord for the way He is using books in these last days. More people read Christian books now than at any time in history. God has put His hand upon the writing and distribution of books He wants men and women to read. I'm thankful to have a very small part in what He is doing.

But these are written, that you may believe that Jesus is the Christ, the Son of God, and that by believing you may have life in His name (John 20:31 NIV).

————————

FEAR FOR CHILDREN

It was through my divorce that I experienced salvation, my first encounter with Christ. Then fifteen years later, one of my sons was sent to prison. As a result of this painful experience, I received the Baptism in the Holy Spirit. Another son's alcoholism brought me to understand God as my loving, Heavenly Father. Then God used still another son, my youngest, and his involvement with drugs, to deliver me from a sick fear about my children and the terrible things they were doing.

I had this fear deep within me, in my mind, and grief in my spirit. I knew I was a Christian, yet I had this awful fear that was nearly destroying my life.

After I read *Power in Praise*, it set me to thinking. I saw that everything in my life was permitted by God. I rejoiced in my heart, and thanked God as I had never before been able to do. I melted before God with praise and thanksgiving. I asked Him to purify anything that would hinder His working through me. I gave myself up to Him to do what He wants. I no longer want my way. I want His way.

God really honored my prayer. He literally turned my mourning into joy and set my feet to dancing. He also filled me with a peace beyond description, and filled me up with Agape love. To me, it's wonderful. I just can't stop praising Him and thanking Him for all that He has done for me. He really does want us to have His joy.

My Comments

God permits only those events which He knows will help us. If in our ignorance or stubbornness we fail to trust Him, we can lose those blessings and suffer much longer than we need to. If we try to figure out how a problem can eventually benefit us, we may be able to think of nothing. But God is not limited to our feeble minds. He can deliver us from the prison of fear.

For my thoughts are not your thoughts, neither are your ways my ways, declares the Lord. As the heavens are higher than the earth, so are my ways higher than your ways, and my thoughts than your thoughts (Isaiah 55:8-9 NIV).

HUSBAND OVER-WORKS

In my line of work, I frequently run into problems. It's my job to find the solutions. My work is demanding and I've always been very good at it. I take pride in my ability to "produce." Unfortunately, my work often requires me to be away from my family at inconvenient times. I've felt it was my responsibility to "bring home the bacon" and it was my wife's responsibility to run the home and take care of the children. When I came home from work, I felt I had a right to relax and not have to face problems - after all, I did that all day at work.

I thought my wife was happy with our marriage, but now she has left, taken our children, and says she is considering divorcing me. Reverend Carothers, there are many women who would be really thankful to have a husband who would provide financially for them as I have for my family. We have a very nice home, live in a good area of town and my wife has never had to want for anything. Yet she claims I've never been a "real" husband and father. As I sit here writing you, I realize that there are ways in which I probably have neglected my family over the years. Yet I've worked hard to provide good things for them. Please pray for God to work a miracle for us. I want my family back. Should I thank the Lord they are gone?

My Comments

Like Martha, this man has been busy doing many good things, but has left the most important thing undone. His first responsibility was to love his wife sacrificially, as Christ loved the Church. Jesus gave His life for the church. He could give no more. This man has not given his wife the love that she needed. Rather, he gave her what he wanted to give. Their children are now suffering from his mistake, but it may not be too late.

God has given him - and us - this opportunity to see that He also wants our love more than our works. This experience can lead us into a glorious understanding of the grace of God.

If we husbands give our wives and children our love, but are unable to supply all their material needs, they will stand by us and be willing to help. If we give God our love, He will always be there to help us.

As this husband and father thanks God for the breakup of his home, the Lord will teach him things that he needs to learn. God's power is released in our problems when we thank and praise Him that things are exactly as they are. When we submit to His dealings with us, we grow in Christ until we reach that place where we can sincerely pray "Not my will, Lord, but yours be done in my life."

I will restore to you the years that the locust hath eaten (Joel 2:25 KJV).

———

I KNOW THE REASON

I am confined in jail under a charge of armed robbery. I read in a philosophy book once that "to live is to suffer; to survive is to find a meaning in the suffering." I have found that meaning.

I am thirty-two years old, have served time in three different penal institutions, and am an alcoholic. I tried AA, read many books on Eastern religions and Yoga - all without success.

I came to Mississippi the first of this year after being out of prison in Kentucky for eight months. I immediately got involved in starting a drug-rehabilitation program. My ambition was to be of some help to first offenders, to keep them from going to prison by getting them probated to our program. I was very successful in my work, and felt that this was what God wanted me to do. Somehow, however, I started drinking again. As a result, I am back in jail. To say that I was ready to give up would be an understatement. I knew God had a purpose for me, but I couldn't understand why He had let this happen. I was sorry I had been born.

Then two of your books, along with a handmade cross, were sent to me by a close friend of my mother. As I read *Prison to Praise*, I identified with many accounts throughout the book. Previously, I thought I had exhausted every avenue, every possibility of finding a meaning and purpose for my life. But reading your book made me realize that I am where I am because *God loves me.*

What freedom that realization brought to me! It was a real turning point in my life. I am praising God for allowing me to go through, and benefit from, this experience. I am a new person. It's fantastic to think that I had to come to jail to be free, but it is true. And I have an inner peace that is beyond anything I have ever experienced. Praise God and His Son Jesus!

My Comments

The Holy Spirit has shared with this prisoner an eternal truth, that God will use all things for our good if we will believe Him. It is hard for many people to understand, but I know that he can find more peace and joy where he is than most people can find on the "outside." Even most Christians expect to find joy in the things that they want. They have not learned to let God take difficult experiences and turn them into pure joy.

His joy will help him win others to Christ. In hundreds of prisons across the United States, men are seeing a real revival. We, too, can be used of God as we give Him our love and careful obedience.

For Christ's sake I delight in weaknesses, in insults, in hardships, in persecutions, in difficulties. For when I am weak, then I am strong (II Corinthians 12:10 NIV).

WOW!

All I can say is that you put me on the wildest trip I was ever on. When I decided to practice what you teach about praising God, I stepped into a new world. Wow! Is it ever exciting!

My Comments

I wish I could include hundreds of letters that I have received similar to this one. Today is, as one man expressed it, "a new ball game." God is the umpire, as He always has been, but now we know it!

Today I am freeing you from the chains (Jeremiah 40:4 NIV).

A SIXTEEN-YEAR-OLD

I am sixteen years old. I am writing to you because I read your book *Prison to Praise*. It opened my eyes to what's happening with God and the Holy Spirit.

I have been a very jealous person all my life. My girlfriend tried to teach me about God, but it just didn't sink in. I am writing this letter in hopes that you will pray to the Lord for me to become a good Christian. I have sinned so much that it bothers me.

I want Jesus Christ in my life, but I just don't have enough faith. I would like to quit smoking and swearing, but I can't stop. I have no patience at all. I would like to become one of God's children. I would like to receive the Baptism in the Holy Spirit. I go to church on Sundays, but it does me no good. I don't get anything out of it. I want God to work through me. I want to become pure inside, with all impurity removed. I feel like an idiot walking around sinning wherever I go. I feel a deep love for God, but I have never had faith in Him. I never thought that He answered *my* prayers, but I know that He will if I become a child of the Lord. Pray for me.

My Comments

Many thousands of young people are looking for the real answer. The traditional approach of "go to church on Sunday" will never satisfy their needs in today's world. The Holy Spirit is moving all over the land and creating a deep hungering and longing to know God, and to love Him. This young person's letter reflects the hunger for a vital relationship with God that most young people want. Each of us needs to cry out to God that His Spirit will minister through us to meet these urgent needs. It is clear that although young people are engrossed in many kinds of harmful activities, they *want* to find a better way. The doors are wide open for you and me to minister to them.

If you extend your soul to the hungry and satisfy the afflicted soul, then your light shall dawn in the darkness, and your darkness shall be as the noonday (Isaiah 58:10 NKJV).

TRAGEDY?

A ten-year-old little girl had cancer. The doctor said, "We must amputate her arm." Many prayers were offered before the day of the scheduled operation.

One night Jesus spoke to the girl before the operation and said, "You will lose your arm, but you will feel no pain." After the operation, the child proudly and confidently announced that Jesus had taken away all the pain. The doctors and nurses could not believe this, and stood by to give a pain-killing shot when one was needed. Hours went by. And days. The child continued to affirm that she had no pain. Until the time of the operation, her reactions to pain had always been normal. She was a living illustration of God's faithfulness to any promise He gives us.

Weeks later, there were signs of cancer throughout the little girl's body. Many prayers were prayed by family and friends. Some of them were angry. Her father thought, "If God doesn't heal her, then I don't see how I can ever believe in God."

The child grew worse. She read a book called *Prison to Praise* and thanked God for her cancer. As her body weakened, she continually thanked God, and her praise gradually transformed her family. The father grew in confidence and trust that God was working in his daughter's life. He fully expected her to rise up and be completely well. But the child's breath weakened, until with one last effort, she said, "Thank You, God," and she was gone.

The funeral was more joyful than a wedding. Hymns of praise and thanksgiving filled the church. God was honored as the giver of every good and perfect gift.

Afterward the father said to me, "Because of our daughter's sickness and death, we came into the most glorious experiences of our lives.

We had never heard of being baptized in the Holy Spirit. God used our daughter's suffering to help us know Jesus in a way we had never known Him. Previously, we had known Jesus as our Savior. Now we know Him as a close friend. God used what others might call a tragedy to fill our lives with praise and thanksgiving."

My Comments

This father's radiant faith draws others to Christ in a powerful way. People who know him say, "There must be a God who cares, to make this man and his wife like they are."

Yes, God does care, and He permits only those things to happen to us that He knows will bless us and others. The real tragedy is that often people permit themselves to be beaten down by the difficult experiences of life. While they drown in grief and self-pity, the power of God to bring victory goes unclaimed.

I receive at least twenty-five letters a week from husbands and wives who are experiencing what they believe is a tragedy. "My husband has gone off with another woman." "My wife has decided she doesn't love me anymore." With great care, they explain how the tragedy has not been their fault, and how wicked and sinful their mate is. These outcries do not bring them one step closer to victory.

What is the solution? We must all say, "God is with me, and He knows exactly what I need. He is permitting this problem in my life because He knows it will help me realize my greatest need. He loves me too much to allow anything to happen that will not in the future be a great blessing to me."

Is this impossible for you to accept? Then you must live in anguish until you become willing to accept it. It is part of God's plan for your life.

This is not to say that He causes marriages to break up or sickness or death. But He uses our problems to strengthen our faith and to force us to depend on Him. Whenever we become so wrapped up in life that our happiness depends upon another human being, God knows that we need His help. He often permits Satan to inflict whatever havoc is necessary to drive us into a position of trust in Him, rather than in humans. When we have learned what we needed to know, He is able to step in and flood our lives with the joy that recognizes Him as it's source.

I will turn their mourning into gladness; I will give them comfort and joy instead of sorrow (Jeremiah 31:13 NIV).

———————

A DIABETIC

Two years ago, when I was eleven, I had to go to the hospital with the symptoms of diabetes. I accepted my disease and was a well-controlled diabetic. Last October my Mother really got closer to Jesus. One day she asked me if I thought God could heal me, and I said yes. Then she read Matthew 18:19: A*gain I say unto you, that if two of you shall agree on earth as touching any thing that they shall ask, it shall be done for them by my Father who is in heaven.* We agreed that God would heal me. And He is doing it! My insulin comes down little by little. Praise the Lord! God let me get diabetes for a reason, and I really do thank Him for it. My life is an adventure, now!

I wrote you this letter because I wanted to tell you I learned a few things from your book, *Prison to Praise.* I pray for you and I wish you would pray for me, too.

My Comments

Thank the Lord for the faith of a child. We can all learn something from this simple acceptance of God's promise. Candy and ice cream can be pretty important to a teenager, but God will supply all our needs when they are given to Him. This young girl could have endured many months of agonizing hunger for candy and other forbidden foods, but instead, she has enjoyed the peace that Jesus offers.

Out of the mouths of children... You have made perfect praise (Matthew 21:16 AMP).

I THOUGHT I UNDERSTOOD

I read *Prison to Praise* and *Power in Praise*, and I heard you speaking about praising God for everything. I believed what you said, and praising God for everything had become a firmly fixed part of my life.

Then something happened that tore me apart. I wanted to thank God for it, but couldn't. It was the opposite of everything that I wanted for my life. I could see no possible good ever coming out of the situation. No good at all! The only thing I could say was, "God, I am not able to thank You, but I am willing." I kept telling God this through my tears.

Then the impossible happened. God took my problem and used it to work out the most glorious peace and joy I have ever had. Life seems so continuously joyful that I've been literally acting like an intoxicated person. The amazing thing is that this new joy keeps going on and on.

My Comments

If God's promises are only for those who live quiet, undisturbed lives, most of us are out of luck. Trouble and strife seem to be shadows that follow us. But God's promise to supply all our needs are as firm and unfailing as the law of gravity. Put your faith in God's promise to meet your every need, and God will bring peace to you. This is the law He revealed to us through Christ Jesus. Do not be discouraged if you have to go through problems. Personal experience is a far better teacher than anything that others can tell you about God!

No matter how many promises God has made, they are "Yes" in Christ (II Corinthians 1:20 NIV).

VICTORY IN GRIEF

My husband had been an Army chaplain for twenty years when he retired. It looked as if we had many happy years ahead of us. His death from a heart attack was completely unexpected, and it shattered me. I was not prepared for anything like that.

But I learned one truth that came to my rescue. I knew that in God's Word I could find help. Each morning I rose at 5:30, went to the beach, and read the Bible. Verse after verse kept telling me to rejoice, be thankful, and praise God for everything. Within a few weeks, a marvelous peace filled my heart. As I thanked the Lord for my life as it was, He came to me in a way that was more real than I had ever known. I knew I was not alone.

How I praise Him for the wonderful power there is in praise. Please keep spreading the message of thanksgiving, so many others will know peace instead of grief.

My Comments

One person loses a loved one and endures years of agony. Another learns the peace that comes to us through praise. God provided the mystery of electricity to ease man's burdens. For thousands of years, man did not enjoy this luxury - many still do not - although provision was made by our Creator. In the same way, many people still carry their own burdens, though He has provided freedom through praise.

I will sacrifice a free will offering to You; I will praise Your Name, O Lord, for it is good (Psalm 54:6 NIV).

_____

BACK INJURY

I have a problem that I can't solve. We have a forty-seven year old son who has been in the Army since he was eighteen. He had a severe back injury several years ago, and he suffers constantly. He had surgery three times, spent time at Mayo Clinic, and has spent many months in the hospital in his hometown. The Mayo doctors sent him home with a steel brace for his back, and told him they were afraid to attempt any further surgery. He suffers so much.

In your book you tell of many miracle healings. I believe in God's healing power, but as hard as I pray, I can't seem to get through. I am sick too, and have many financial difficulties.

My main concern now, however, is the illness of our son. He has a wonderful wife and four lovely children, but life is hardly worth living when one suffers with every breath.

My Answer

God is also very much interested in your son. Often a parent does not realize that God is using even sickness to help his children. If you will believe that God is using your son's back problem and his pain to help him, this will release God's power to do what He wants to do. If you are fearful and afraid, you hold back the mighty healing power of our Heavenly Father. The natural anxiety of a mother's love will not release the supernatural power of God to bring supernatural healing.

Remember, as you reach out your hand, that Jesus is always there to touch you, and to meet your needs. Please believe and trust in Him.

Christ Jesus ...is at the right hand of God and is also interceding for us (Romans 8:34 NIV).

———————————

IN DEBT

I've been a Christian for sixteen years. I was saved when I was twelve years old. But I have been terribly depressed since my marriage eight years ago. The relationship is not pleasant.

My husband will not stop charging things, and we're in debt up to our ears. He has a good job and is a good friend of the governor of our state. We go to church every Sunday. I teach organ, we both sing in our church choir and teach Sunday School classes, but there is still something wrong.

For eight years, I've lived in a prison, you might say, and now since reading your book, I know there's freedom and happiness for me. I know it lies in Jesus, but I don't believe He is with me.

Please pray for my life and my needs. I feel I can't keep my head up any longer. I praise God for my problems, but I still can't understand why.

My Answer

If nothing was going wrong in your life, you would probably relax and be so contented, that you would not realize your own great need for God.

You find your peace in having things in a good, decent order. If these needs were met, you would not be crying out for God's help. Your spiritual need is great, and God loves you so much that He has permitted the problems that will draw you to Him. If you were out of the human prison that you write about, you could still be in a spiritual prison.

Ask God to fill you with His Holy Spirit. He will help you find great victory in Christ.

He will take your depression, and fill you with His joy, regardless of what your husband does. God will use you to bring new light and understanding to others, who have problems similar to yours.

Since God has given you a desire to be out of your "prison," He has also provided people around you who can help. Seek them and you will find them.

For He has rescued us from the dominion of darkness and brought us into the kingdom of the Son He loves (Colossians 1:13 NIV).

WHY NO TONGUES

Jesus is my Lord. He is with me. Devout and dear Christians have prayed for me, but I still do not speak in tongues. What is wrong with me? Instead of a joyful spirit, I have a sad and sorrowful spirit. I want to speak in tongues and to have a closer walk with my Lord. I believe in the Lord and know all things are possible. Am I baptized in the Holy Spirit, or am I only saved? He heals me, hears me, and saves me, but please, please pray for me. I want more of the Lord's Holy Spirit. My minister tells me that speaking in tongues is of the devil.

My Answer

Praying in the Spirit is an opportunity given to us by God, to believe what His Son promised. Turn to the sixteenth chapter of Mark and find that Jesus gave you a promise. His promise was to give a new language to everyone who "believed." Your problem is you have not *believed* that promise. If the Holy Spirit disregarded your lack of faith, you would never have realized how important it is to believe Christ's promises.

When we fail to trust in Jesus, we do not have a joyful spirit. To disbelieve Him brings sadness. This can happen even to those who have accepted Him as Savior. You can want to speak in tongues, but still be bound by your lack of faith in what Jesus said.

You write, "I believe in the Lord and know all things are possible with God," but in this one thing you have not believed. Like many people, you believe that He is *able* to give a new language, but you do not believe that He has *already* done it.

Please accept His promise and believe that the new language is yours. When you do believe, then in faith open your mouth, and let the Holy Spirit speak through you in words that you do not understand.

Be prepared for the devil to tell you that it is only your imagination. He tells this to everyone. He always wants to discredit everything that the Holy Spirit does. He wants us to disbelieve everything Christ told us.

We have the joyful opportunity to decide whether we believe Christ or the devil. Unbelievers may tell you they believe that speaking in tongues is of the devil. Here again you must decide whether you will accept what men say or what Christ said.

For many years I was uncertain how I should feel toward those who believe and teach that praying in tongues was of the devil. I tried to keep an open mind so that I would not be critical of those who did not believe as I did. Then the Holy Spirit ministered very powerfully to me and said, "You must not remain silent about those who say My work is of the Devil."

I understood, in a new way, the danger anyone places themselves in, if they accuse the Holy Spirit of speaking by the devil. This was the sin Jesus spoke about. He said men could speak against God and against Him, but warned strongly against speaking evil of the Holy Spirit. I therefore speak out against any group or organization or fellowship that says speaking in tongues or the Baptism in the Holy Spirit are of the devil. You should have no part of them, give them no encouragement or assistance in whatever they are doing. I am not speaking against any person, or group of believers, who disagree with us. I am speaking specifically about any group that openly condemns the Holy Spirit and declares His work to be of the devil.

There are many who do not yet understand the working of the Holy Spirit, and for them I have only love and understanding. They are praising God and worshiping Him as they understand

Him. I encourage you to help, love, and hold them up to God. He loves them and wants us to love them. People do not have to agree with us in theology and in practice, in order for us to have blessed Christian fellowship with them. I am only led to be directly and positively against any person or group who considers the working of the Holy Spirit to be the work of the devil.

I tell you, every sin and blasphemy will be forgiven men, but the blasphemy against the Spirit will not be forgiven (Matthew 12:31 NIV).

GOD CHANGED MY IN-LAWS

I have read all three of your books, and I'm going to read *Power in Praise* again. It was the most difficult of all the books for me to accept. But on looking back, I realize I was not trusting God. Although I believed in Jesus, I was afraid to allow Him to handle my life.

What I wanted was a made-to-order Jesus who would jump to my commands and do all I asked. Now I understand what the centurion meant when he told Jesus he was a man of authority, and subject to authority. I have been in the service long enough to know that a good soldier will not question the validity of his commander's actions. He does what he is told.

Because he trusts his commander, he trusts that whatever his commander does can be trusted.

In the same way, I should not order Jesus to do anything. I should present my needs to Him, and since He is my commander, I should trust that He is taking care of *everything*. There is no joy in questioning the Lord in what He does, but what a joy to put my trust in Him. When I look at my problems, I see God working in everything for my good, once I have surrendered my problems to Him.

I want more information on how I can help in the Foundation of Praise ministry. I am a Methodist also, and have studied a little about the beginning of the Methodists. This ministry to the souls in prisons and hospitals sounds very much like the ministry of John Wesley and the early Methodists.

For a long time, I have been praying for my older brother and his wife, and my younger brothers, that they will become Christians. Now I have surrendered them to the Lord for His safekeeping. I know He is taking care of them.

I have been praying with my wife for her parents to accept Christ as their Savior. For quite a while her parents had been nearly at each others throats. The tension was terrible. My wife was so upset she was in tears whenever she talked about the bitterness between her parents. We finally agreed that, because we had been praying for Jesus to touch them, God would work some good out of all of it. We thanked God for taking control of the situation, and in five minutes we felt God's Spirit touch us and fill us with a wonderful glow and peace. We knew God was at work!

The next day my wife went to her parents' home to do laundry. She said her parents were strangely happy, relaxed, and the atmosphere had changed - no more tension, but peace and love. We know the Lord is beginning a breakthrough in their lives. Every time we see them, they are happier than the last time!

Praise the Lord, Brother Carothers! I praise Him with you! He is a great God. How wonderfully He cares for us all.

My Comments

It is a very beautiful thing to see the simple, childlike faith of this serviceman. He has comprehended the beauty there is in turning our problems over to God and trusting Him. In our twentieth century society, we have become accustomed to doing everything for ourselves. We feel compelled to solve every problem and to right every wrong. God, in His mercy, permits us to experience situations that we cannot change.

In these situations, we learn to turn to God and to trust in Him. He will do what we cannot do. He wants us to have faith in Him, not in ourselves!

Throughout the Bible, God looked for men and women who would believe Him. When He found them,He accomplished marvelous things. If you want to be well-pleasing to God, accept the opportunities He gives you to show your faith in Him. Remember that you were born where you were, and when you were, as part of God's plan for you. He knew, even before you were born, the nature of the problems you would have. He could have stopped your birth, but you were being prepared for His eternal use.

This young soldier knows that no commander wants to have people around who complain and groan over the situation. The good commander is aware of what is going on in his unit. He wants the people under him to trust that he is doing the best he can. God, our Commander, wants us to believe that through Christ He is working in all our problems. The Holy Spirit does not bring His fruit of joy to the heart that is grumbling against God. If you want joy and peace in your life, be thankful and praise God for everything, and the Holy Spirit will do His part.

In Your presence is fullness of joy (Psalm 16:11 NKJV).

BABY WOULDN'T SLEEP

From the day we first brought our daughter home from the hospital, she had never slept more than three or four hours at a time. She was often awake all night and then fitful all day. She never slept more than eight hours a day from the day she was born and usually only about six hours a day.

The doctors could give us no explanation for the tense, upset disposition she had for the first two years of her life.

Then I heard you talking on the radio about praising God for everything. I had never heard of such a thing. I was rocking our daughter as you talked, so I decided to try what you were saying. I thanked God for our baby just as she was. I thought of the dozens of sleepless nights and agonizing days she had given us. I thanked God for her, as she twisted and squirmed on my lap. Suddenly, she relaxed and fell asleep! I put her in her crib and she slept for twelve uninterrupted hours! I could hardly believe it.

That was several weeks ago, and ever since she has slept for twelve hours or more every day. When she is awake, she is as happy as any baby I have ever seen.

Words cannot express how thankful I am to God. I don't understand what happened, but it had to be a miracle.

My Comments

There are spiritual forces working in this world, about which many Christians are unaware.

Restless, unhappy people roam all over the world not knowing about the peace Jesus came to bring. This mother touched the source of that peace when she entered into praise, and released God's power to work a miracle for her little child.

And He (Jesus) *took them up in His arms, laid His hands on them, and blessed them* (Mark 10:16 NKJV).

———————

MY GUEST WAS LATE

Thank you! Thank you for your book *Prison to Praise*. What a blessing! The Holy Spirit has truly used it in my life. For the first time, I can praise the Lord for all things without feeling as if I'm lying. I read your book a little over a week ago. Since then, my world has turned upside down as I praise Him for things that had previously made me unhappy. I see life in such a different light.

By the way, I read your book in four hours, while waiting for a friend to arrive. We hadn't set a time for her visit, but it was getting late, and I was angry, thinking she wasn't coming. I thanked the Lord for my anger and for her not coming. Then I realized she wasn't going to come until I finished the book. That's just what happened. We had a wonderful visit. I shared your book with her and thanked the Lord for His marvelous plan.

I could go on and on, but I wanted to share what your book has done for me. There are many things I need to overcome. Now I know I will, because *God's* timing is right.

My Comments

I am often asked how we can thank the Lord for our sins.

In order to thank the Lord for sins, we must first recognize the sin. It would be difficult to thank Him if we have not confessed it. We can be thankful for the sin only if we believe God is going to work something good out of it. I have known people to flippantly acknowledge a sin and carelessly say, "Praise the Lord." If anyone adopts this careless attitude, he is overlooking a very important part of being thankful to God for all things. The Scripture promises that God will work out all things for good to *those that love God.* Loving God is a very important part of praising Him and being thankful.

If we love someone and realize that we are doing something that hurts him, what are we going to try and do? Loving him requires that we do our best to keep from hurting him. We would, therefore, strive to find some way to help that person. If we love God, we will do everything possible to keep from becoming involved in anything that we understand to be wrong. Anything less than doing our best shows a lack of love.

We should not allow ourselves to fall into condemnation when we have done the best that we know how to do. Even for human beings that we love, we can only do what we are able to do. Beyond that, we must trust God and believe He will make up for what we cannot do.

We must be in harmony with the Scripture that says, *Whatsoever your hand finds to do, do it with all of your might* (Ecclesiastes 9:10 KJV). Our Christian living requires that in the midst of our praise, we show our love for our Heavenly Father.

If you love Me, keep My commandments (John 14:15 NKJV).

───────────

MY MOTHER

I'm filled with thanksgiving for your two books. I will explain why. My mother runs a house of prostitution. For several years I have lived in such shame and self-pity that I have not wanted to go outside my own home. My husband's work is in this city, and we could not leave. I felt like a prisoner in my home. I was ashamed to go to the grocery store or even to church. I felt so ashamed of my mother. My dear husband kept telling me that it wasn't me, so I shouldn't keep thinking about it. But I couldn't help myself.

I prayed often for God to deliver me from the horrible burden, but it wouldn't go away. Then a friend gave me your books. I laughed and cried as I read them. A beautiful peace came into my heart as I realized that God could take even my mother's present occupation and use it to do something good. I really believe that He is going to lead her to Christ. I am very thankful that God is doing something for my mother.

I now go outside our home with joy and a song inside my heart. I no longer think of my problem. I think of what God is doing. God has used you to bring a marvelous change in me. My husband also thanks you, for his life is changed. He has a new wife. Everything about our home is transformed. I no longer sit around feeling sorry for myself. I know that God is truly blessing me with everything good.

My Comments

This letter gives those who have problems with their family something to think about. As you meditate on what God has done for this daughter, perhaps you'll see that He can do marvelous things for you, in the situation in which you find yourself. God has promised to use everything for our good - if we will trust Him. Satan was using a mother's life to destroy a daughter's peace of mind. Now a daughter is using her praise and faith in God to destroy Satan's work and to draw her mother to Christ.

The reason the Son of God appeared was to destroy the devils work (I John 3:8 NIV).

A CAB DRIVER

Peter was angry, bitter, filled with resentment, and he had good reason to be, from a human standpoint. He was in a prison that had a church member as its cornerstone.

When Peter was twenty years old, his parents operated a small bakery in Brooklyn.

They worked hard, and by frugal living had put their three boys through high school.

A friend in their church said, "You should expand your bakery so you could hire someone to work for you and not have to work so hard yourselves."

The idea sounded good to Peter and his brothers, so they encouraged their parents to expand the bakery. None of the sons worked in the business, and they wanted their parents to find a way to take it easier in their old age. Further talks with the man in the church revealed that he was willing to lend them the money. They borrowed from him and expanded the business. Everything looked beautiful. The sons rejoiced that their parents would soon be able to relax a little and hire someone to do the hard work.

When Peter's parents made the first payment on the loan, they tried to figure up how long it would take to pay the loan off. They were confused when they discovered that after the first payment, the total amount owed was greater than the amount they had originally borrowed.

"How could this possibly be?" they asked the man who had loaned the money.

"This is what you agreed to on the papers you signed," was his only answer.

They kept making the payments, but the amount owed and the interest due continued to grow. Eventually, the burden became so heavy that they lost the entire business to their fellow church member.

Peter lived with his parents and supported them by driving a taxicab. His bitterness and anger grew year after year. He says, "I lay awake at night thinking up things I could do to that church member who had robbed my parents. The only reason I didn't do anything to him was that I could never think of anything bad enough for what he had done to my parents."

Whenever anyone got into Peter's cab and started any kind of conversation about religion, Peter would pull to the curb and say, "If you want to get out, okay, but don't talk about religion in my cab."

The parents grew in bitterness as they faced life-long dependence upon their hard-working son.

One day a man left a book on the seat of Peter's cab. He was gone before Peter realized the book had something to do with religion. *Prison*, he read. Then he thought, "That's where that church member would be if there was any justice in this world!"

Because he had nothing better to do, Peter glanced through the first page of *Prison to Praise*.

The plot interested him, so he kept reading until another passenger got into the cab. Throughout the day, he read whenever he was free. By late afternoon, he had completed the book and God had reached his heart. Bitterness flowed out with his tears, as he asked God to forgive his own failures.

"God, for ten years I have hated that man. I see now that You have used him to bring me to Christ. Please forgive him and me. Thank You for what he did."

Peace so filled his mind that he yearned to share his new understanding with his mother and father. After dinner that evening, he was sitting in the living room with his father, silently praying for God to show him how to share his discovery with his parents. Just then there was a knock on the door, and his father went to answer it. There stood the man who had robbed them of the business! They hadn't seen him for ten years.

"God has made me so miserable and guilty that I have had to come and beg your forgiveness," he said.

The son's heart leaped for joy. God had already answered his praise. But the father was unmoved and silent.

"Your bakery has grown and prospered. It is worth several times what it was ten years ago.

God has told me I must give it all back to you. Here are all the papers you need."

The son could hardly believe his ears. How could God have moved so quickly? When he looked at his father, he knew that a greater miracle had happened. Tears of joy were running down his father's face. The bitterness was gone.

Peter's family is now prosperous, but more importantly, they are a family filled with praise. Yes, the heart of man is deceitful, but God is still able to melt the most stubborn - if we trust Him.

For all have sinned and fall short of the glory of God, and are justified freely by His grace through Jesus Christ (Romans 3:23-24 NIV).

A THIRTEEN-YEAR-OLD SPEAKS

I am thirteen-years-old. I received the Baptism in the Holy Spirit two months ago. But I didn't have any joy because I was letting my father depress me. My father is hard of hearing, and he has bad nerves - which make him talk continually. I couldn't ever talk to him.

Was I ever blessed when I read *Prison to Praise*. It is the most inspiring book I have ever read. Thanks to you, I'm thanking God for a father like mine. It works! The situation is so much better. I am so grateful. Thank you for the great help you have given me. May God bless you and keep you.

My Comments

I do thank the Lord for the remarkable ease with which children often step into a life of praise and thanksgiving. I urge you to tell children about the wonderful joy there is in praising God for every difficulty. They may be able to help you put into practice what you already believe.

From the lips of children...You have ordained praise (Psalm 8:2 NIV).

MY HUSBAND DIED

A short time ago I read *Prison to Praise* and *Power in Praise*. They have been such a blessing to me, and I want to share my experience with you.

Last Christmas evening, my husband and the husband of a dear Christian friend were killed in an airplane crash. The accident remains a mystery, but God in His mercy has given us many indications that this was part of His wonderful plan.

My husband loved the Lord with all his heart, and served Him faithfully. His home-going made a strong impact on many who needed to make decisions for the Lord. We praise Him for this. Our children ages 12, 10, 9, and 6 continually grow stronger in the Lord. Though our loss is great, our blessings and cause for praise far exceed our loss - when we keep our eyes on Jesus.

Your books helped me conquer a great battle. My husband had been flying a private plane, and I had a secret fear of his flying. After the Lord took him, Satan began to cause me to be bitter and to question why, especially when I would see or hear a small plane overhead. I would become tense and begin to grieve again. I knew this was wrong, and I had to have victory over it.

After reading your books, I thanked and praised the Lord for the airplane. Now, whenever I see a plane, I take it as an opportunity to praise the Lord. I ask Him to keep using the wonderful testimony that my husband had.

It does work! Satan's efforts to fill me with bitterness have been defeated through the power of praise.

My Comments

Many people allow the death of a loved one to make them bitter. When this happens, they influence everyone around them. Without wanting to, a parent can cause children to resent God. The tragedy of doing this is beyond our power to comprehend.

When we lose a loved one, it is essential that we turn our loss over to God and trust that He is working in our lives. He will bring forth a beautiful plan for the care and guidance of those left behind.

Satan could take your doubt, fear and frustrations, and use them to work havoc. But through your *faith*, God can and will do many wonderful things.

Precious in the eyes of the Lord is the death of His saints (Psalm 116:15 NIV).

A BILL COLLECTOR SPEAKS

I'm so happy, I'm giddy. God is truly blessing me and using me in a wonderful way. I feel clean and beautiful inside, all because He loves me.

I gave my employer *Prison to Praise*. He told me how much he was enjoying your book but could hardly believe all the miracles in your life.

My reply was "Yes, isn't it wonderful!" He knew of the hardships I had been having in the past.

His attitude has changed, and he thinks God is using you in a wonderful way.

I told him I had been witnessing to our clients. He said that if I wanted to witness to them to take them into the front booth and take my time with them. Before he read your book I'm sure he wouldn't have liked me doing that. Every day has been full of joy.

Every time I give one of your books away, I'm filled with joy. I just seem to bubble over. Right now I want to jump up and down.

This afternoon a client's grandmother called to plead that I stop attachment against her grandson's wages. I wouldn't budge until she said, "We will have to trust in God." I have put *Prison to Praise* in the mail to her, and another copy to her grandson.

My Comments

Too many people try to keep their faith in Christ outside their business life. If a business is such that we cannot let Jesus be a part of it, then I believe we are in the wrong business. The writer of this letter has experienced the joy of letting her testimony minister in her everyday life. He has promised to honor us as we honor

Him. He will keep His promise.

The Lord declares ...Those who honour me I will honour (I Samuel 2:30 NIV).

A PRISONER WITNESSES

I am serving a two-to-ten-year sentence for drugs. I know that God brought me here so I could be freed and find Him. I was born again and baptized in the Holy Spirit one year ago, here in prison, as I read *Prison to Praise*. I have been praising the Lord ever since and working for Him, telling everybody the Good News.

The Lord has used me to win two converts so far. We are working together in the Lord, to try to bring more convicts to Christ. We need your prayers.

It is true that when you thank and praise God for everything that happens, He blesses you, and fills you with joy. I thank God and praise Him for bringing me here so that I could find Him.

My Comments

I ask you to join with me in prayer for all those who have accepted Christ while in prison. The number is rapidly growing. Please visit the men and women who are in prison. Take books that will lead them to accept Christ. God has already promised to reward you.

When did we see You sick or in prison and go to visit You? The king will reply, I tell you the truth, whatever you did for one of the least of these brothers of Mine, you did for Me.... Come, you who are blessed by My Father; take your inheritance, the kingdom prepared for you since the creation of the world (Matthew 25:34, 39-40 NIV).

A CHILD SPEAKS

I will be thirteen the 26th of this month. Last night I read *Prison to Praise* and found it wonderfully helpful. I told God that I would try to praise Him in all things. At certain parts of your book, I stopped and praised God that I had a chance to read your book. Sometimes there would be tears, and I knew God was trying to tell me something.

I don't understand it all, but I believe.

My Comments

Often it takes the simple faith of a child to comprehend the deepest spiritual truth. When we believe something that we do not understand, we demonstrate the faith of a little child. The intellect nearly always wants to override the Spirit, and it is the intellect that gets us into trouble. Our spirit has the potential of coming into harmony with God's Holy Spirit, and it is to our spirit that God is now releasing a new understanding of the victory that comes to us as we enter into a life of praise.

I tell you the truth, anyone who will not receive the kingdom of God like a little child will never enter it (Luke 18:17 NIV).

A BEAUTIFUL DIAMOND

I read *Prison to Praise*. It was beautiful. In some parts I laughed, and in some I cried. I'm writing to you because I need God's help. First, let me explain my life.

I had sex with my cousin when I was only nine years old. I married when I was thirteen, got pregnant one month later, and we separated after four months. I was going with other boys, even when I was married. My husband was still married to another woman. After I was married, I had sex with married men and with my husband's uncle. I even had it with children, for which I am ashamed. I went to bed for money - once even with a woman. I stole and smoked pot. Once I lived with several men and boys at the same time. Surprisingly, most people didn't seem to know what I was doing. Everyone thought I was just pretty and a good girl.

I know now what a dirty life it was. I caught syphilis. I've taken shots, but it's still in my blood, and I worry about it.

I married again at fourteen, but we were separated after only one month, when I found out that he was a homosexual. I married again at twenty-three, and at the same time went out with three other men. My third husband divorced me last year. He then married his fourth wife.

After my divorce I began drinking terribly, cussing all the time, and finally got an ulcer from the way I was living. I was drinking so much that the doctor said it would kill me if I did not stop.

I had never been in love with a man, but would live with one for a month or so and then leave him. I stayed with one man, though, for a year, drinking about eighteen cans of beer a day or until I was too tired to drink any more. A few weeks ago, I was admitted to the hospital because of a bad blood clot in my leg. Just before my trip to the hospital, a man came to all the apartments in our building. He wanted to have a Bible study with us. I laughed in his face.

When I got back from the hospital, a neighbor gave me a copy of your book *Prison to Praise*.

It changed my way of thinking, and I began to want God in my life. I telephoned the man who wanted to have the Bible study, and he came to see me. I had a wonderful time hearing about the Bible. Although I had been serving Satan, I had a deep down feeling that I belonged to God. I would not play games with Him, because I knew that would be wrong.

Thursday, after the first Bible study, I prayed. I asked God to remove the devil from me like you had prayed for the woman in your book. I asked Him to let Christ and the Holy Spirit into my body. While I was praying, my feet became numb, as something was drawn up through my body. My chest was so tight I could hardly breathe. Something seemed to come out my throat, and almost choked me. All the time, I was still praying, and crying. I went blank as I kept repeating, "He has accepted me! God has accepted me!"

I came to myself, crying and saying, "God has accepted me." I felt so beautiful and happy. But I still have problems. Sometimes I feel that God has not forgiven me. I did so many terrible things. I pray to love God, and His children - to really love them. I pray not to hurt anyone with words, or talk about anyone. I pray to love those who do things to hurt me, and to forgive them. I want to love God and have faith and work for

Him. I want to be filled with the Holy Spirit and be ever thinking of my Savior and my Heavenly Father.

Please pray for me in Jesus' name. I do believe He will help me. Maybe I don't have enough faith. The Lord knows, I don't know what it is. I am thanking Him just as you said in your book. I do not question why - I just thank Him.

My Comments

It was my great joy to have the opportunity to pray with this woman in person. It was a most thrilling thing to see her being filled with the Holy Spirit. The life that had already been so dramatically changed was changed even more. Her past life was immediately put to good use. She knew many people who were downtrodden and filled with sin, and she understood them. Her love for people was overwhelming. Her days were spent in witnessing and telling people what Christ could do for them. There was a magnetism about her testimony that drew people to Christ. The old hardness was gone, and a new radiance shined all around her. Many people accepted Christ because of her testimony, and many are still being drawn to the Lord.

It is easy now to thank God for everything He

permitted to happen in her life. He took a crude lump of coal and refined it into a beautiful, shining diamond. God will throughout eternity hold her up as an illustration of what His Son Jesus has done for a human being.

Therefore if anyone is in Christ, he is a new creation; the old has passed away, behold, the new has come (II Corinthians 5:17 RSV).

PRAISE THE LORD

Your books have been a great blessing to me. The Lord has helped me learn to trust Him.

After my second daughter was born, I had a real battle with postpartum depression. I never wanted the child, as I had my own ideas of when we should have another baby. My husband was very patient through my pregnancy and stayed by my side even in the delivery room.

We were having many financial difficulties, and though we could hardly feed ourselves, my husband was constantly giving to others. Well, you can imagine the fit this unsurrendered Christian threw!

Our second daughter was a cranky baby, and I was cranky right back at her. Her sister was never like that, and I had prided myself on having such a good child. My husband said our first child was so good because we loved her so much, and our youngest could be too if we would love her. I would never harm her, and every now and then I mustered up some motherly love. I even prayed that Christ would love her through me. But I didn't really love her myself.

When my husband left me, I had peace, but I didn't praise God for the situation. As I asked God to guide me, I understood some of the reasons why my husband left. I confessed them to God, but, oh, so righteously! I knew I must do something. Then I read your books. The very instant I began reading, I got a blinding headache and tightness in my chest, as if all my sins were coming to a head like a boil. I always had a head knowledge that my situation was for good, but never a heart knowledge.

I realized for the first time that God had let my husband leave before I could do anything more to hurt him. I praised God for that in thankful confession. I began thanking Him for everything - even the endless round of dirty diapers. I can't figure out their good, but I know in my heart that even dirty diapers have a purpose, so I am thankful.

My husband still isn't home, but I have peace that soon he will be. I know I can't divorce him as I planned. I must love him with Christ's love and pray for him and ask his forgiveness. I rest assured that this family will be united again in God's good time. Not when my husband has changed, but when I have been changed and am more thoroughly schooled in walking in the Spirit.

Our baby is still a crab, especially now that she is teething, but to me she's a precious little crab. I love her with Christ's love, and that's all I need. My husband comes to visit a wife who praises God for dirty diapers, spilled milk, ruined makeup and even vomiting on the freshly shampooed rug.

I still don't feel overflowing joy at all my tasks, but I am convinced it's because my feelings have ruled me for too long. I have glimpses of that joy and am overwhelmed at the prospects. The cloud gets thinner every day. I am convinced that whole and healthy families are God's will. I am praying for just that and the patience to wait, and the submission to praise Him without looking for a quick result.

The headache and tightness have almost left. Any time I seek God, I have a fight with Satan. Won't it be great when he has to stay in hell! Isn't it great that Christ in me has the final victory! Praise the Lord!

My Comments

This letter is a beautiful commentary on the wonderful power there is in praising God. So many families are torn apart by the great difference in human personalities. When one party or the other becomes overwhelmed by the stresses of life, he is usually cut off from the joy that God wants to give us. This wife has discovered the wonderful reality that no matter what happens, God wants to work everything for good in our lives. The normal reaction is to blame everything on the other person, but she is learning to accept the changes God wants to bring in her own life. This acceptance is producing in her a peace that rebellion can never bring. Her recognition that praising God does not always bring instant results, has contributed to her faith in God's working out His total plan.

Too often, people give a quick try at praising God, and then flee back to self-pity when they think it hasn't worked.

This wife has realized that often God permits a separation or even a divorce to save one of His children from destruction. A distressed husband or wife may, by indulging in over-possessive love, be refusing to allow God to take care of the ones that He loves. If we truly love someone, we must be willing to let go and let God work out their life in whatever way He knows is best.

Rest in the Lord, and wait patiently for Him. Do not fret... (Psalm 37:7 NKJV).

FROM A PRIEST

I thank you for the inspiration I found in reading *Prison to Praise*. I am uncertain about many things in myself. I'm often misled and end up in a dead end. I know God loves me, but I am discontented with myself and have a poor self-image. I feel resentful toward my peers - jealous, afraid, up-tight - and always seem to be running away from myself. I put up a front often of being other than I am, and have a real battle with thoughts and imaginations.

I was prayed over for the Baptism in the Spirit a while back by some Catholic Pentecostals, but I still bear these mixed-up feelings and really freeze. I'm afraid to open up.

Your faith seems so strong that I'm encouraged to ask you to pray for me for a healing in these matters. I have a few hang-ups with impure thoughts and desires; I am fearful of my feelings, and fearful that I'm not doing the Lord's work - feeling compelled to fail. At times

I even doubt my calling. I don't feel my heart is in my life. Perhaps the devil is trying to trick me into looking too much for natural fulfillment. I need balance.

I know I should praise God for my life, as confused as it is. I've been ordained many years and feel it's time for a conversion of heart. I need to be pushed in the right direction and to keep ongoing. I'm always afraid of souring the situations I am in. I think basically I'm afraid of women (with all of my imaginings), somewhat closed to men (unhappy and unwilling to share), and I don't have enough discipline in my life.

Can your faith help me? I seem afraid to live - the opposite of you - although you do share (rather you *did* share) my feelings about getting up in the morning.

I really want to get Jesus across to people. I need His Spirit, but I feel chained to my self and sometimes become too clerical and businesslike (dead is the word). Like Lazarus in the tomb, I stink! Praise the Lord, He can raise me up. Please pray for a brother in need so that he can be numbered among those who have felt God's power working through him.

My Comments

I have omitted from this letter details that

might reveal the identity of this brother in Christ. I include his letter to help you to see that problems are not limited to those who earn their living in the secular world. I also want you to recognize the great need there is to refrain from criticizing a member of the clergy who seems like Lazarus in the tomb. Men who recognize a deep spiritual need often do not know what to do about it. They should not be criticized, but loved, no matter how cold or how unspiritual they seem. Do not take for granted that his heart is satisfied to remain where it is.

His letter reveals the deep cry that is often in the heart of a pastor as he longs to be of greater help to his people. Your love for him could be the very thing that will lift him into a new dimension of praise. As God uses your love and kindness toward him to set him free from bondage, His potential for leading others to Christ will become much greater than before. I do not mean that you are compelled to remain under the ministry of someone who is not building your spiritual life, but you can, as the Spirit leads you, minister to those God has brought into your life. You can go out of your way to express your love and concern for them even when they do not seem to respond.

I continue to pray for the priest who wrote this letter. I invite you to join me in prayer. One day we will hear that God has filled his heart with the joy he so earnestly longs for.

Now glory be to God who by His mighty power at work within us is able to do far more than we would ever dare to ask or even to dream of-infinitely beyond our highest prayers, desires, thoughts or hopes (Ephesians 3:20 TLB).

IN THE WILL OF GOD

Thank you for your books. They helped me so much, through so many trials. And especially when other Christians acted as if terrible things were happening to me because I was out of the will of God. I felt so discouraged and as though I had no faith at all. Then I would read your books, begin praising God, and feel the joy of the Lord return.

Lately our prayer groups had teaching on binding Satan many times every day. Every time I get involved in these teachings, I feel fear coming back. When I know God has control of every area of my life, and I praise Him, my fears disappear.

My Comments

Many people fix their attention on Satan. Our attention should be fixed on the One we are following! He is leading us out of where we have been, into a new place. He does not want our attention on the past, but rather on His future for us. Jesus is worthy of all our attention, all our praise, all our love!

The Lord is faithful, and He will strengthen and protect you from the evil one (II Thessalonians 3:3 NIV).

BUSINESS FAILED

I started a business that I expected to be a big success. But I didn't select my three partners carefully enough. The business I knew and understood, but people...? I don't understand them.

One partner was slovenly and lazy. Another argued all day. The other stole everything he could sneak out the back door.

Now tell me the truth. Do you think I should praise the Lord for the people who ruined my dream?

My Comment

Ruined his dream? People don't do that! We can only do that to ourselves. We decide how other people's actions will influence us. We *decide!*

Another man had a dream. He was an

inventor. Several men recognized his ingenuity and offered to invest in his ideas. They formed a company, with the inventor as president.

The company prospered. The inventor's ideas worked. But the investors grew impatient. The work wasn't progressing as quickly as they anticipated. They thought the inventor wasn't working hard enough. He spent too much time "thinking." Eventually these investors forced the inventor out of the company and they took over. They even controlled his patents.

The inventor's dreams were temporarily interrupted. But he still had his dream and he kept working. His name? Henry Ford.

Blessed and happy is the Christian who learns to not be controlled by what other people say or do. God is in control! He permits certain people to come into our lives! He selects them! The people we need, do to us what we need, in order to force us into the position where we can learn God's will. If that sounds strange to you, remember Joseph. He needed to be in Egypt to do the work God called him to do. Therefore, God used his evil hearted brothers to sell him into slavery.

Does God work as intimately with all His children? He says He knows the numbers of hairs on our head! He knows when a sparrow falls. He knows every thought we have. Oh yes, He is involved in every detail. When we understand that, we are free! Whatever any man or woman does to us, it will work *for our good if we love God* (see Romans 8:28).

Some readers of this book have been carrying an ache in their hearts, over something someone else has done to them. They may have been hurting for years. Now is their opportunity to be free!

Believe God permitted that person to do that thing to you, that you might now learn how to submit your heart to God. If we allow other people to trouble our hearts, we are indirect disobedience to His will! Why not enjoy obedience!

Let us examine our ways and test them... Let us lift up our hearts and hands to God in heaven...For His compassions never fail, they are new every morning. Great is your faithfulness (Lamentations 3:22-23, 40-41 NIV).

IT ISN'T FAIR

Why was I born? Nothing goes right for me. Hardly anybody likes me. I have no talent. Whenever I try to accomplish anything, someone stops me. My health is terrible and I look worse. How can I praise the Lord when there is *nothing* to praise Him for?

My Comment

The Apostle Paul lived in horrible circumstances, but he refused to be defeated, or even discouraged. Because he trusted God and had learned to be content regardless of his situation, Paul was able to rejoice in the Lord and be at peace.

Happiness on this earth does not depend on our circumstances. If it did, many of us would be in trouble.

There is a big difference in the way unhappy and happy persons treat their circumstances. One person suffers *under* them - the other stands *on top* and shouts, "I've won!"

Why is this? Stronger will power? Better health? More advantages? More talent? Better looking? No! The difference is that some folks have learned the secret - others haven't.

Paul was one of those who had learned! He decided that God was on His side! What a partner! And since GOD was on His side, it didn't matter to Paul, who, or what, was against Him (see Romans 8:31).

Paul decided that since God had already sacrificed His own Son for our benefit, He wouldn't fail to supply everything else we need (Verse 32).

Paul *believed* in God's love, therefore, to him

everything that happened was a blessing from God. So, whatever occurred, Paul climbed up on top and shouted, "Victory!"

No one could say Paul lived a sheltered, protected, luxurious life, or that his generation applauded him. No way! We love him, but in those days most people avoided him!

Paul attracted trouble. The majority of the unsaved didn't like what he said - or how he said it. His former associates wanted him dead. His new Christian friends often turned their heads whenever he was in trouble.

Paul's reaction to all of this? He knew that Jesus was at God's right hand. What did he see Jesus doing? Paul said, "He's praying for me!" (Verse 34). And since he knew that, he mocked troubles. Persecution, famine, nakedness, peril or even a sword could do only one thing - help him! (Verse 28)

But notice in verse 37 that Paul wasn't just a conqueror. He was more than that - far more. Why? He knew how much Jesus loved him! This is the difference between people who live *under* the circumstances and those who live *on top* of them.

Paul was so exuberant in his faith that he claimed victory over: angels, principalities, powers, the future, big problems, little problems and even including, "Anything ever created!" (Verse 39).

Paul refused to be separated from God's love, no matter who did what, or when (Verse 37). He would not accept any event as misfortune or bad luck.

That's the secret, dear troubled friend. Our confidence in God's love decides our reaction to every experience in life. If we believe God loves us, and pays close attention to everything that happens to us, we shout, "Victory" at *every* turn of events.

No one can do this for us. Each of us must take off the blindfold, open our eyes and go for it. I can help you a little by telling you my own experiences. The problem is this: If you have been living *under your circumstances*, you may resent any interference in the way you run your life.

The writer of the above letter classified many things that were wrong in his life as, "their fault" or "God's fault." He - and any of us who are like him - must take our attention off anything that might prevent us from understanding God's love for us.

We must learn to love God. This is a proven way to understand God's love for us! Do this by:

1. Telling Him the reasons you love Him. This isn't for His benefit! It's for yours.

2. Finding dozens of occasions daily to tell God how much you love Him. Sing about it.

3. Taking your attention off anything that

separates you from God. Turn off television, movies, radio, records, novels, magazines, etc. that are not produced by men or women who love God. Otherwise your mind will be polluted by those who will (without you realizing it) separate you from God.

4. Concentrating your attention on God's Word. Many have learned to love God by knowing what He has said and done. Learn to hear God speak. That's not easy, and it requires your full attention. No time to be wasted!

5. Finding people who love God and are learning about His love for them. They will assist you along your way.

6. Don't give up. Your goal is too important.

Since I began learning about God's love for me, so many good things have happened. My health improved. God gave me better and more loving friends. My opportunities to help people have increased. My joy keeps increasing. Every time Satan slips in some evil device to threaten me, and I stand on top of it, my joy takes a new leap upward. I want to help all men to *mount up on wings like an eagle* (Isaiah 40:31).

The more I believe in God's love for me, the greater joy I experience. He loves me not because of who *I am*, but because of who *He is*.

Over the past 2,000 years, Paul has had more influence in the world than any other follower of Christ. Whenever God finds a man or woman who relies on His love, He uses that person.

Believe in, trust in, and rely on God's love for you. The more we do this, the more blessed and favored we will feel *and be*!

May they...know that you sent me and have loved them even as You have loved Me (John 17:23 NIV).

———————————

You will also want to read these other best-sellers by Merlin R. Carothers

Prison to Praise $5

Many people list as the most unusual book they have ever read. Millions say it changed their lives and introduced them to the solution to their problems. This is not a book about a prison with bars, but about a prison of circumstances–and how to be set free!

Prison to Praise, Read on CD $16

Power in Praise $9

Learn how the principles introduced in *Prison to Praise* work in every day life.

Power in Praise, Read on CD $16

Answers to Praise...$9

Overjoyed Christians felt compelled to share with Merlin the "signs and wonders they experienced while practicing the teachings in his first two books

Walking and Leaping $9

When Merlin and his family rolled over a hill in their new car and trailer they praised the Lord and miracles happened!

Bringing Heaven into Hell............................$9

Merlin shares new discoveries of how the Holy Spirit sheds light from heaven in the midst of a personal hell.

Victory on Praise Mountain......................$9
Spontaneous praise often leads into valleys that are direct paths to higher ground.

The Bible on Praise.................................$4
A beautiful front cover painting by Merlin. Features Merlin's favorite selected verses on praise from thirty-eight books of the Bible.

More Power to You $9
Written for people in every day places who need more power in their every day lives.

What's on Your Mind?..............................$9
Would you be ashamed for everyone you know to see your thoughts? If so, you urgently need to read and understand *What's on Your Mind?*.

Let Me Entertain You $9
After years of serving the Lord Merlin was eager to retire. He wanted to rest, relax and enjoy a quiet life, but God had other plans for him.

You Can Be Happy Now $9
Everyone desires to be happy! This book will help you to understand how much God wants you to be happy.

From Fear to Faith..................................$9
God wants to be intimately involved in your life and help you have victory over your problems.

Secret Sins $9
As you read this book you will be especially pleased to learn that God has provided a simple way for many of us to be delivered from our secret sins.

God's Secret Weapon $9

How do we find true, lasting happiness? How can we endure suffering and tragedy? The answer is a powerful weapon and is available in this book.

Amazing Power of Faith................................$9

Many people do not know the correct answer to the question," Are you going to Heaven?" Read this book to find the powerful answer.

AWARD WINNING MOVIE

A true story based on the book with more than 15 million copies in print!

A First Place award by "National Religious Broadcasters."

An Angel Award by "Excellence in Media."

A First Place Covenant Award by "The Southern Baptist Radio and Television Commission."

ISBN 987-0-943026-39-3

If you didn't believe in miracles before, you will after watching *Prison to Praise*.

A sixty minute DVD that will be enjoyed by both children and adults.

Available for $10.00 from:
Foundation of Praise
PO Box 2518
Escondido CA 92033-2518

Please enclose $4.00 for shipping on all orders

221

About the Author

Merlin R. Carothers' books have been translated into 58 languages. A Master Parachutist and Demolition Expert in the 82nd Airborne Division during three major campaigns of World War II. At the conclusion he served as a guard to Gen. Dwight D. Eisenhower. Later, as a Lt. Colonel in the U.S. Army Chaplaincy he served in Europe, Korea, the Dominican Republic, Panama and Vietnam. He is a pilot, lecturer and retired pastor. He has made many appearances on national television and has traveled worldwide to share what he has learned about praise.

At the age of 89, on November 11, 2013, Veteran's Day, Merlin was 'promoted' to his heavenly place.